WALL AND ROOF CLIMBING

including useful appendices on interior, tree and haystack climbing

GEOFFREY WINTHROP-YOUNG

author of 'The Roof-Climber's Guide to Trinity'

They tell me if I climb and stand
   Upon those distant ledges,
I shall but see on either hand
   Dim fields and dusty hedges,
But yet I know my fairyland
   Lies somewhere o'er these edges.

ALEXANDER

OLEANDER PRESS

The Oleander Press
16 Orchard Street
Cambridge
CB1 1JT

www.oleanderpress.com

First published by Spottiswoode and Co., Limited, 1905
This edition published by The Oleander Press: 2010

A CIP catalogue record for the book is
available from the British Library.

ISBN: 9780900891854

Designed and typeset by Hamish Symington
www.hamishsymington.com

Printed in England

TABLE OF CONTENTS

Introduction i

Chapter One: Rock versus Roof I

Chapter Two: Literary History... 20

Chapter Three: Women Climbers 53

Chapter Four: Material and Architecture 63

Bibliographical II5

Appendix A. II6

Appendix B. I22

Appendix C I26

"You must go to Shiny Wall, and to the white Gate that never was opened; and so you will come to Peace-pool."

CHARLES KINGSLEY

"And as he was troubled thereabouts, he saw two men come tumbling over the wall...

Chr. Why came you not in at the gate which standeth at the beginning of the way?

They said that to go to the gate for entrance was by all their countrymen counted too far about, and that therefore their usual way was to make a short cut of it, and to climb over the wall as they had done...

They told him, that custom, it being of so long a standing as above a thousand years, could doubtless now be admitted as a thing legal ... and besides, said they, ... we are also in the way that came tumbling over the wall."

JOHN BUNYAN

INTRODUCTION

> "For those
> Who would see Virtue in her proper sphere,
> Now climbing of a wall."
>
> C. BROOKE

Contributions to the serious literature of Climbing are never complete without a foreword. A critical examination of the text has however revealed no statement veracious enough to call for the customary apology. Objection might perhaps be taken to a certain indiscriminate use of the terms "roof climbing" and "wall climbing." Their relative positions should indeed excuse an identification, for the roof forms the almost invariable finish to wall ascents and is itself "technically" unattainable save by their means, but the indefiniteness rests also upon historical grounds. It has been found impossible, owing to the lack of contemporary record and the studied neglect of later historians, to discover in what period the art of wall-climbing merged itself in that of roof-climbing, at what date the aerial junction of distinct wall-homes opened those fair fields for practice beneath which degenerate moderns cower for protection. That a Wall Age existed is all that is known, and Byron epitomises the whole knowledge:

> "Pronounce who can! For all that Learning reaped
> From her research hath been that there were Walls."

The history of the transition of the art from its exercise on these mural structures to its orophismic reappearance in

> "The golden bowers of Shadruchiam
> And the diamond turrets of Amberabad"
>
> *Lalla Rookh*

is sufficiently ill-determined to excuse an involuntary vagueness in descriptive terminology.

Attention has been drawn to one important omission, the absence of the 'caution,' inevitable in such works, to all whom it may concern not to do the same. The correction shall be as succinct as it is customarily superfluous.

Firstly to those on whom the progress and safety entirely depend, the Builders. Let them strenuously resist the economic enticements of the mutual-supporting street and the architectural giraffe, for

> "Houses are surest, which are not builded high,
> Whereas high buildings may no tempest endure,
> Without they be founded sure and steadfastly."
>
> BARCLAY, *Ship of Fools**

Recognizing their own direct responsibility for every misfortune, let them see that their work is firm, irregular and in all

---

* Cf. Horace: "Celsae graviore casu / Decidunt turres."

respects suited to its real object: briefly, let them

> "Build to-day then strong and sure
> With a firm and ample base,
> And ascending and secure,
> Shall to-morrow find its place.
> Thus alone can we attain
> To the turrets."
>
> LONGFELLOW, *Builders*

Above all, let them keep ever in mind that:

> "no fair colours,
> Can fortify a building *faintly* jointed."
>
> FORD, *Broken Heart*

Secondly, to those emulous yet nervous aspirants who complain, "Fain would I climb, but yet I fear to fall," we commend Queen Elizabeth's corrected reply, "If thy heart fail thee, do *not* climb the wall."

Youthful and confident climbers, who burn to establish their reputation by some sensational 'mill-chimney' ascent, should mark the advice of the *Faithful Friend*:

> "A desperate man,
> That climbs a tower whose top the wind ne'er touched.
> Must chary be, lifting his resolute foot.
> Or headlong down he comes."
>
> FLETCHER

One caution more, to that numerous class of experienced climbers, who, in their anxiety to display their strength and speed, too often bring destruction upon their supports, human and edificial: let them recollect that, however admirable may seem to them the fierce resolution of the Roman senators —

> "We'll *break* our walls
> Rather than they shall 'pound' us."
>
> *Coriolanus* I. 4

yet a great poet and a sincere stegophilist has emphatically pronounced those alone "wiser, greater," who show themselves

> "*Gentler* than they
> Who on the fragments of yon shattered dome
> Have *stamped* the sign of power."
>
> SHELLEY

Finally, be it remembered that since experiments must necessarily be conducted principally upon the landmarks of our neighbours and the privileges of the fox-hunter have not yet been popularly conceded to the climber, it is well to evince a modest unassertiveness of time, place and motion, and whether our essays be upon the Welsh ruin, the family obelisk, the roadside railway-arch, the rococo bank-facade or the continental market-fountain, Chu Hsi's maxim should constitute our motto:

> "When mounting the wall of a city do *not* point with
> the finger,
> When on the top *do not call out.*"
>
> *Learning for the Young*

A list of graded international Problems, which it had been intended to include under the headings of Problematical, Highly Problematical and Absolutely Hypothetical, threatened to assume such vast dimensions and yet remain incomplete, that it has been thought better to leave the classification to local effort and a serial publication.

The indispensable Bibliography, Technical Appendices, etc., will be found at the end, and a Song of the Brotherhood suitable for Club Dinners.

CHAPTER ONE

ROCK VERSUS ROOF

"We have not wings, we cannot soar,
 But we have feet to scale and climb
By slow degrees and more and more
 The cloudy summits of our time.

"The mighty pyramids of stone
 That wedge-like cleave the desert airs.
When nearer seen and better known,
 Are but gigantic flights of stairs."

LONGFELLOW

The hardly achieved peak is now no longer the summit of the climber's ambition: let him but be on the point of publishing, and the height of his desire is attained. It is a road, though it be that of fame, yet a road alone which his heart yearns to tread. To him the Pyrenees are a stout octavo with illustrations; the Andes flit before him, a glorious quarto vision, thirty-two-shillings-with-maps: Europe is being ransacked for un-Ruskinised aiguilles, and every stone in our own land stamped with a name and perpetuated in a guide-book, yet no disquisition has appeared upon wall or roof climbing.

It is no part of our purpose to dilate upon its fascinations, to dwell on the delights of a stiff brick "back-and-knee" chimney, or the pleasures of a "free-backed" water-pipe. To those who do not know them we can only say, – try! It is the most attractive and most economical branch of the climber's art, a branch within reach of the lowest of us and one which permits the enthusiast to enjoy the fruits of his labour with the least possible preliminary exertion. Let some of those contemptuous stay-at-homes, who are perpetually dinning in our more adventurous ears their gratitude for possessing, and their desire of retaining, a roof over their heads, make trial of the charms of feeling one beneath their feet, and if they cannot cry with the ancients "The heaven is my roof," they will soon be compelled to acknowledge 'the roof is my heaven.'

Yet it is well to premise that these encouragements must not be taken as general incitements to rash attempts upon the severer climbs. We should be the last to advocate attempting the difficult ascents too soon, regarding the Psalmist's utterance as of all-pervading importance, "it is but vain labour that ye haste to rise up so early."*

False pride is an intolerable rope-mate; and the gods

---

* "Pythagoras bounde all his schollers to five years silence, so that assoone as ever they crept from the shel they might not aspire to the House-top." Gosson, *School of Abuse* (1579).

themselves, if we may trust contemporary tradition, thought no shame to grade their attempts to their abilities:

> "An hospitable roof they found,
> A homely shed, the roof not far from ground,
> From lofty roofs the gods repulsed before
> Now, etc."
>
> DRYDEN, *Baucis and Philemon*

No less accommodating at the present time are the supernal gradations; and in roof architecture, even more than in the Swiss Alps, it is possible for the uninitiated to penetrate into the very heart of the grandest and most sensational scenery with absolute security. There are few buildings that do not admit of some means of access to their higher plateaux, and it is these lower summits, these Aeggischhorns and Rigis of the domestic hearth, whose attractions are urged here upon the attention of those who —

> "ask no more,
> No tip-top turret whose aspiring brow
> Looks down and scorns the humble roof below"
>
> J BROME

those who can find contentment on low leads — subject of course to conditions of weather and the kitchen chimney.

But to those whose aspiring soles would rise to loftier levels, an additional word of caution is due. Roof-climbing is no child's play, and the local mill-chimney is not a fit practice ground for the anxious novice. It is an art distinct in itself:

that which gives it its chief charm, the variety of roof forms and the infinite number of materials employed, wood, brick, stone, concrete, iron, slate, chalk and lead, also constitutes the chief danger. There are no guides here to judge for us by instinct of the bearing capabilities of a given material. Years of practice are required before an adequate general knowledge of their qualities can be secured, knowledge which must ever be open to modification and change to suit the circumstances of age, climate, or the builder's honesty. That earliest of educational authorities, Sir Henry Wotton, lays down indeed the broad lines of a graded course in the wall arts. He would have everyone "to pass a *running* examination over the whole edifice after these premises, if the house be found to bear his years well, then let him suddenly run *backward* from the ornaments, etc., etc."* This course might be adopted with striking results by all beginners. In most cases the rapidity of the consequent progress will be surprising.

ROCK *VERSUS* ROOF.

The great feature which distinguishes roof-climbing from rock-climbing and renders its pursuit difficult, not only for the beginner but even for the mountain expert, lies in the abruptness of the angles. Even in the Dolomites, whose ledge and chimney effects most closely resemble the straight-line architecture of the builder's ideal, vertical walls are rare, and generally permit of evasion or relentingly disclose some vulnerable

---

* Elements of Architecture

crack. But the builder exults to show his superiority to Nature and his contempt for her soft-hearted methods. His walls are as straight as plumb-line can make them, his tiled or slated gables maliciously turn all their holds the wrong way, his chimney-stacks emulate the intellectual development of the Early Victorian high hat. Wonderful is the difference two or three degrees make in the rapidity and security of the young climber's progress. We have known a confident Alpinist, who could gambol over the Pillar Rock, lose his character in a brick chimney overhanging a fifty-foot wall, and even skilled roof-climbers, obstinately applying their saxan methods to the altered condition of the angles, become pounded by walls that yield easily to more jut-icious devices.

It must not be concluded that there is therefore no resemblance between rock and roof climbing, and that proficiency in the one is of no assistance in the practice of the other. As a matter of fact there is a curious parallelism between their natures, which, if kept constantly in mind, will enable many a difficult problem to be solved by analogy. The contemptuous Balbus will boast of the firmer lines and finer finish of his work, unconscious that the relation of the mountain to his wall is much that of the race to the single man, who passes rapidly in his short life through all the stages of development and change attained in long ages by his kind. When Nature first began upon the mountains, she was a Bloomfield in her prejudices and ideals and a Scott in her callousness to the needs of future climbers. She hurled up vast and impregnable edifices, she adorned them with threatening rock-courses and palaeolithic barge-boards, she plastered the whole with a generous facing of ice, and there from amid machicolated gendarmes and colossal turrets of smooth and unscalable granite she looked forth defiantly upon an indignant world, wrapt like the inaccessible Rapunzel in her golden tresses of cloud.

But fortunately Nature was compelled to admit her arbitrary measures wrong, and to acknowledge that her jerry-building was not constituted to resist the peremptory conditions of time and weather. The cheap ice proceeded to peel off, furrowing the rocks and ruining the surface in its course, the soft upper strata rotted and fell, and the carefully laid lower ones got mixed and jumbled lowering the mountains to half their original height — a vast relief no doubt to the troglodytes of the time; such an edifice as the Borrowdale volcano, vouched for by a local guide-book as 30,000 feet high "on the authority of the oldest inhabitant," can but have been regarded as a nervous neighbour by the lacustrians in a high wind and its subsequent disintegration hailed as a happy despatch.

Consequently Nature had to set to work again, and she weathered back the walls to a good safe angle, and drew ledges and traverses across the faces to catch the falling stones and strengthen the rotten rocks, and she buttressed up her pinnacles with gloriously sharp bastions and arêtes, and she gouged out gullys and channels for the water to escape down, and finally flung over all a protecting curtain of glacier and snow. And the modern architect goes out and looks upon the rugged results and he smiles at Nature; but the roof-climber smiles at the architect; for he has visited the innermost recesses of his work and he knows how ephemeral and insecure are the results produced by the greatest names and how even the best are only unconscious imitators of Nature's methods. He sees that the cheap plaster is but the peeling ice, that there is only the difference between convex and concave 'twixt the gully and water-pipe, that the string-course, the gable, the projection have all their mountain original, and that the insecure roof-gutter but too closely resembles the frail ice-cornice. And he knows (or he ought to know) that Nature, with time and weather more wise than the architect, is always endeavouring to improve the likeness and indulge the climber, that

> " Time decays
> The strongest, fairest buildings we can find."
> FLETCHER, *Temple of Honour*

In time the plaster will scale off, exposing a rough surface or granting a foothold, the dried mortar will fall out or yield readily to the finger, the heavy walls will lean and convenient cracks open, and iron bars and buttresses be needed for many a chimney-stack and turret; while, like their alpine prototypes the hanging glaciers and the snow-couloirs — keys to many a hopeless ascent when all other means have failed — over all will slowly spread the heavy creepers.

It is not necessary here to continue the parallel further. Younger generations of climbers may, if they will, extend and follow it into its more scientific branches; sufficient has been said to show that it does exist and, apart from its inherent interest, may prove of considerable service to both schools. If it is allowable to quote an instance, we ourselves for years, with the true faith at heart, scorned a waterpipe as adventitious aid in spite of the halo of respectability and romance draped round it by the youthful Lord Clives ecclesiastical exploit. Consequently until the close parallel of the gully, that highway of the mountain fraternity, was revealed, the climbing field (field is an unsuitable word, but it is less cockney than area) was cruelly confined. Now, however, there is an old friend in every pipe; their collar fastenings appear 'pitches' of the most interesting character: few pleasures are equal to proving a match for their devices – for all pipes are full of tricks, not all easy to smoke even when light is thrown upon them – and no Scotsman could finger them with truer delight. Still another instance may be found in the story of the roofite who was long puzzled by an alluring ruin, until, remembering the rule to which reference will be made later, that the sun is to the building what no-sun or shade is to the mountain, he sought for his sheltered snow-patch on the sunny side and found it in a noble Wistaria.*

Although naturally at first the younger art must gain a larger

---

* Cf. also Bishop Heber: "I crept beneath thy tower, / I climbed the ivy tree."

profit from the greater experience of the elder than it is able to bestow, yet the advantage gained by comparison does not lie wholly upon the side of roof-climbing. In future years, no doubt, proximity and facility of practice will reverse the positions, but even at present the exchange is becoming more mutual: —

> "Nec celsas soliti ferire turres
> Ardentis via fulminis movebit."
>
> BOETHIUS, *Cons; Phil.* I.

The story is well known of the *Herr* who declined to allow his guides to attack what is now known to be an impossible face, "because," he declared, in the parlance of the roof arts in which he had graduated, "a good south wall that hasn't a creeper, weed or lichen in autumn to show for it, must certainly be new mortared, probably stone-faced"; that is, in Alpine English, "A sheltered north face that hasn't either ice or snow upon it after the winter storms must be without ledge or hold, perhaps consists of the much-dreaded 'Platten.'"

Allusion has been made above to the 'sun-for-shade' rule. It is a law of opposites. What shade is to the mountain, sun is to the wall. This cannot of course be pressed too far, but it will often prove useful in application. In snow mountains the side exposed to the full heat of the sun is the one to be avoided, where the snow slopes may have been turned to ice and there is the greatest risk of avalanches; the sheltered side proves as

THE SUN-FOR-SHADE LAW

a rule far safer, with its rocks firmer and its snow-slopes more frequent and more secure. In walls, on the contrary, it is on the sunny side, where "branching from the brickworks cleft" the creepers and grass-tufts grow, where also, if it be brick, the mortar will be loosest and the face most broken up, and if stone, the grips will prove firm and dry and body friction be increased. So too in house climbing it is the sunny side that indulges most in the welcome balcony and sun-shutter, and offers many a grateful step on sun-blind rollers and fastenings or on the fragile ice-glaze of a south view trellis work.

A curious proof that this was a recognised rule even in the earliest ages survives in the now misused phrases of its being best "to look on the bright side" or "to be on the sunny side of the wall." And an even more interesting confirmation exists in the very ancient ballad of the *Demon Lover*:

> "Oh what hills are yon, yon pleasant hills
> That the sun shines sweetly on?"
> "Oh, those are the hills of Heaven," he said,
> Where you shall never win."
>
> "Oh, what'n a mountain is yon," she said,
> So dreary with frost and snow?"
> "Ah, yon is the mountain of hell," he said,
> Where thou and I wilt go."
>
> Percy *Ballads*

Here we have the lady, devil or author, which you will, on the first sight of the mountains at once applying the traditional wall-climber's rule, that "where the sun shines lies the heavenly way up." Had he, she, or it possessed a knowledge of hill climbing equal to their knowledge of wall scaling, they would have known that wall laws hold in mountains exactly in their opposites, and the snowy or un-sunned regions could not but have appeared less infernal to them. The error however points a useful moral to modern hill-men too apt to repeat it in the converse direction; and the verses themselves are an invaluable proof of the acknowledgement of this law by the Climbing Fathers.

Indeed, though Wall and Roof Climbing are dealt with here as new arts, and in their later scientific developments practically are so, yet it is incontestably proven that wall scaling is certainly coaeval with man, probably a survival of the monkey. Even in the garden of Eden additional guardians were necessary to prevent infringement on the mural enclosure*, and the Devil alone knows how long the annual celebration of "Wal-purges Nacht" by primordial witches – as the word indicates, a sort of "Scouring of the White Horse" – has continued. But to the ancients the wall was more than a mere back garden trapeze, on which they might indulge their simian propensities. It became in time a necessary part of their

---

* Gen. iii. 24. See also Marlowe: "Now walk the angels on the walls of Heaven." *Tamb.* II. 24.

lives and was used, not only for purposes of pleasure* and entertainment as we see in the still extant word 'party-wall,' but as a citadel to which to retire; the long misunderstood phrase of "the weakest to the wall!" being clearly the warning cry raised upon sight of an invading foe. Their confidence in these mural defences seems to have been on the whole justified. Even in the oft quoted case of Jericho the walls yielded only to the distinctly artificial aids of the trumpeting Jews. In later times this custom of retirement grew upon them, and the constant references to 'walled cities' show us that for greater security they took up their residences permanently upon the summits, "where," we read, "of ledge or shelf the rock rose clear, or winding stair." The very word 'to walk' is obviously derivable from the original practice-ground of the then new art of locomotion. The somewhat precipitous approaches presented no more difficulty to our ancestors than an ordinary front steps, and even babes in arms — to recall the little elegy:

> "Over the garden (guardian?) wall
> I let the baby fall"
>
> *Nursery MSS*

— manifestly proved no prolonged encumbrances to their jumping-jenny-like mothers. These were the dawn-golden

---

* The "Waltz" was the rotatory dance executed on these narrow heights, as contrasted with the "Square" or "Country" dances, suitable for town or forest levels.

days of the wall, when the Celestials were raising their colossal exercise structure, the Great Wall of China[*], and before the roof had begun to settle upon its edges. Kings walked upon it[†], Homeric gods thought no shame to build it, the Babylonians drove their chariots and hung their gardens along it, the world spent its time attacking or defending it, when demi-gods "whistled the march tune, 'Warrior to the wall,'" and Hector κέκλετο δὲ Τρώεσσι ... τεῖχος ὑπερβαίνειν. History, briefly, was the mortar of its joinings.

Besides this utilitarian employment of its powers we find in the case of the Tower of Babel, and in both Tacitus and Gibbon, additional evidence of the early origin and existence of the climbing wall or obelisk purely *ad hoc*. In Gibbon's words, "In a remote but polished age, which preceded the invention of writing, a great number of these obelisks were erected, in a just confidence that the simplicity of their form and the hardness of their substance would resist the injuries of time and violence. In later ages several of these were transported to Rome by Augustus, Constantius, and the Emperors."[‡] This notice is of great interest as indisputable evidence of the

---

[*] The Chinese have a great climbing past: the Pagoda is one of the most perfect developments of the Problem. We read that, "From time immemorial Wall-literature has been a feature in the life of a Chinese city, surpassing that of any other nation." *Chinese Literature.*

[†] 2 Kings vi. 26, 2 Sam. xi. 2, and Marie de France, *Lay of Eliduc.*

[‡] Cf. Goldsmith: "As in those domes, whom Caesars once bore away." *Traveller,* 1st edit.

existence of a classical stegology, and an important proof of
the climbing value set upon the erections of the early wallites,
whose miniature Babels were sought for by the Emperors as
private parlour Alps.

The obscure cautions so frequent in Horace:

> "Nec tibi prodest,
> "Parcius junctas quatiunt fenestras
> Aerias tentasse domos!"
> Ictibus crebris juvenes protervi."

in Claudian:

> "Speculamur ab altis
> Turribus *incerti!*"

and the later Augustans, viewed in this light acquire a new
significance.

The opinion used to be widely held that wall-climbing was
confined to a few distinct tribes, and was by no means general; and in support of this view was quoted the evidence of
the comparatively few and now widely dispersed names sur-
viving which bore reference to it, such as Wallachians, Wal-
denses, Walloons, etc., the very fact of their existence being
claimed as a proof that the custom was considered sufficiently peculiar by their neighbours to win for its practisers
distinguishing titles. The reverse however is now maintained
by the younger school of critics. With greater probability
they declare that the custom was universal among all peoples

however named, and that these names are no more than terms of abuse or nick-names which, as is the way with nick-names, have long outlived even the memory of those who earned or gave them. Their very rarity they quote as evidence of the otherwise universality of mural skill. Thus the Wal-lachians obviously were destitute of their neighbours' most highly-prized possession; the Wal-loons can have been but sluggards at the art; and the Wal-denses need but a two letter change, easy to the philologist, to stand before us in the peaked head-gear of their shame.

A few personal proper and improper names also survive, titles perhaps of individual distinction or dishonour. Thus a 'wal-lower,' word suggestive even now of grovelling, must have been looked down upon by his tribesmen of higher position; the original Waldorf was clearly too exclusive; Waller or Walter, the word is the same with different terminations and is identical with Murphy, must have been considered a cragsman of note; Cad-walla's methods seem to have been unpopular with his climbing contemporaries; and much doubt exists with regard to the family names of Wallenstein and Stonewall Jackson as to whether they refer to the unusual material employed in their ancestral crows'-nests or to their hereditary method of running their heads against them.

Some would find in the people of Wales (as of the Canton Wallis) a nominal survival similar to that of the Hausas in Africa, others again have the audacity to claim William

Rufus as a believer. In an earlier age the Malmetine laws, very properly originated by a son of the suggestively named king Dun-wallo, ordained the making of a "high way of stone and mortar from Cornwall to Caithness." The enthusiasm of the former county, which earned it its name, no doubt gained for it also the distinction of possessing the starting point of this famous "high level route." Alas that so little knowledge survives to us of its employment!

Among the black races of Africa or the Pacific, with their defective building arrangements, but small survival is to be expected. Yet Christopher Brooke claims even here a constant popularity for the art:

> "What walls are these that to sad eyes discover
> Such subtle weeds, whose fabric is hung over
> With Blacks?"
>
> *Chichester*

Similarly "altes Haus"* is still the greeting of affection among our co-Anglo-Saxons. And while 'a stony heart' or 'skin flint' are terms of reproach and a 'stonewaller' is looked on as one who puts a stop to everything, on the other hand our language contains few words of warmer praise than that Climber's Delight, 'brick,' and Mr Jorrocks might have known no insult could have been intended by the obviously faithful one who hailed him as "old bricks and mortar."

---

* "An old and crumbling House best suits my tread." YOUNG

The facts and causes of the gradual shifting of the diluvian residential mansions from the wall to the the roof are only conjecturable. Some attribute the change to the general 'Volkerwanderung' and the consequent evolution of the staircase[*], others to the accidental discovery that the conjunction of two walls by their mutual collapse upon one another gave greater freedom of movement on their summits. The latter supposition is strengthened by the form of Cheops' pleasureground Pyramids. These solid pinnacles, explicable only as climbing problems[†], with their sloping, joined sides, half wall, half roof, are invaluable specimens of this Transition period. More accurate information is unobtainable, and the almost imperceptible beginning of the finer art of roof-climbing is without record. Even after the transformation the roof forms retained impressions of their slow chrysalis stage, similar to the gables and domes of modern desirable mansions; as we learn from Gibbon: "The edifices in form were simple and oblong, rarely swelling into the shape of a dome, sometimes branching into the figure of a cross, and all covered with tiles of gilt brass." That these last had defence as their object is certified from Greek sources:

"Πᾶσα δ᾽ Ἄρη κεκόσμηται στέγα

ALCAEUS

---

[*] "The Tartar scouring the steppes of Central Asia." FARRAR

[†] "Set me to climb the high Pyramides, / I'll either rend it with my nails to naught / Or mount the top." MARLOWE, *Massacre at Paris*

The roof had replaced the wall as the citadel of defence, and in such stormy times was a much frequented locality, needing elaborate protections. At a later date, when defence became happily of secondary importance, much ingenuity and treasure were expended on adorning and rendering secure these favourite resorts. What says King David?

> "Therein be neither stones nor sticks,
> Neither red nor white bricks ...
> There is goodly sardonyx
>   And amber laid in rows.
> It goes round about my roofs ...
> There is good space for horse and hoofs,
>   Plain and nothing perilous."
>
> SWINBURNE, *Bersabe*

Traces of the habit are still noticeable in the kindred races of the East, where the earnest householders spend most of their days and nights upon their roofs, and naturally have endless opportunities for practice and perfection.

In our own country scanty record remains of this early roof history. Up to the present day indeed the survival has been more in individual exploits than in general favour. Certain classical and widely used phrases serve to show us that the practice did however continue to exist, and that vigorously enough for its phraseology to become a part of speech. Thus 'to slate' implies the abuse the original deserves for its noisy frailty. To be 'a flat' suggests the want of those irregularities of humour or gabling so pleasing alike to the dinner companion and roofite, and no greater distrust can be expressed in the upper storey of the human being or the house than to hint that there is a 'tile loose.' In spite also of the opinion of some modern critics who profess to find in the lines as they stand some trace of Goth or Vandal influence*, we are inclined to assign to this obscure era of tecto-murality that most exquisite of all wall love-lyrics:

> "Oh wally, wally up the bank
> And wally, wally down the brae
> And wally, wally yon burn side
> Where I and my true love up gae."

---

* The Vand-als were a notorious walling tribe [Idg. Wand=N.E. wall]. The Goths, as their architecture witnesses, had a trained climbing eye: "The Goth was stalking round with anxious search, / Spying the time-worn *flaws* in every arch." BURNS

CHAPTER TWO

LITERARY HISTORY

"Where the terraces ran, there did we run:
Where the towers curved, there did we curve."

DE QUINCEY

We have said that the wall and roof traditions were for centuries chiefly supported by individual effort. The full list of these pioneers would be exceedingly long and heavy, including as it does innumerable names famed both in literary and actionable spheres. The school of Eton has the glory of claiming the training of many of these our honoured chimney-jacks; so at least we gather from the frequent notice in their biographies that at Eton they were "famous at the Wall game."* But the distinction was not confined to one school or one class; Clive won it on his church, Byron on his

---

* The College roofs formed apparently the scene of operations: in the 15th century there was a daily dispersal after dinner for practice: "Some to Chamber, some to Bower [Brewer?] / And some to the High Tower." *Life of Ipomydon*

steeple, the gentleman in grey-worsted shorts in his cupid-like ascent, Humpty-Dumpty in his unfortunate descent, the Regent of France on his window-grating, Jean Valjean in his obtuse-angled corner, and Love no doubt several million times through his window*. Many of those who may have shunned the practical sky-light, found outlets for their stegological sympathies in their writings. Thus, in Shakespeare's most human play, Wall occupies a sufficiently remarkable position, and is saluted with many endearing synonyms, as 'Mural,' 'wittiest Partition,' etc., but it is even more significant that the author has centred all the dramatic interest and all Pyramus' affection in the '*chink*'. So also Tennyson, assuredly another sympathiser, lays a reduplicated emphasis on the fact that it is "flower in the *crannied* wall."

It is indeed interesting to note, both as bearing on the history of our subject and illustrating the peculiar refinement of its ethical content, that the chief exponents of the art and the principal recorders of its attractions have been throughout the poets. Ruskin and certain of the classical philosophers form notable exceptions, and among the historians Carlyle relates of himself, "On the coping of the orchard wall, which I could reach by climbing, ... my porringer was placed; there many a sunset have I, looking at the distant western mountains, consumed, etc." But in the main it would seem that

---

* This proverbial feat has however the confirmation of only one discoverable eye-witness: "Then saw I Love upon the castle wall." LORD VAUX

the fascination has been stronger for the sensitive few of the idealists than for the grosser masses of prose writers.

From a scholarly point of view this is to be deplored; for the history compilable from poetic reference must necessarily be of a subjective and intermittent kind. The allusions only serve to indicate indirectly the continuous nature of the influence, and their interest lies principally in the personal lights which they cast upon the individual characters. A few citations from these unsatisfactory historical *Quellen* should be permissible, as confirming the fact of the antiquity and the extent of the inspiration. It will be noticed even in these scanty examples, proportionally selected, how they multiply with advancing centuries. The boast of our transatlantic brother seems indeed not unlikely of fulfilment:

> "Day by day, o'er tower and turret,
> In foul weather and in fair.
> Day by day in greater numbers
> Flock the poets."

LONGFELLOW, Walt v. d. Vog.

CLASSIC PERIOD   In the Classic Ages Homer[*], Euripides[†], Alcaeus[†], Aristophanes[†], Lucretius[‡], Catullus[†], Horace[†], Virgil[†], Claudian[§],

---

[*] *Il.* xii. 468

[†] See text and elsewhere

[‡] v. 7

[§] *De nupt Honor*, v. 87 seq.

Statius*, Lucan†, Plautus†, Seneca‡, Boethius†, and others† all exhibit after their various manners affection, such as Aeschylus' for his "φίλαι στέγαι," or belief, such as Ovid's, that

"Fama tenet summaeque domum sibi legit in arce."

v. 39.

Aeschylus is in despair at the curtailing of his rambles:

"I at a loss am left
Where I may turn, for the house is falling."

Euripides lingers over Hercules' prowess, when

"Up he climbs and down along the roofs,"

and the *Orestes* abounds in luminous passages:

"ἴα, τί χρῆμα; λαμπάδων ὁρῶ σέλας
δόμων δ' ἐπ' ἄκρων τούσδε πυργηρουμένους":

again:

ἢ τῷδε θριγκῷ κρᾶτα συνθραύσω σέθεν,
ῥήξας παλαιὰ γεῖσα, τεκτόνων πόνον."

ἐπὶ τὸ τέγος ἀναβαίνειν is a motto for both Xenophon and Thucydides, and a very early recorded ascent is borne witness to by Herondas in the *Mimes*:

---

* *Silv.* v. 131

† v. 400

‡ *Tro.* v. 2

23

"If we venture to scold him the young rascal perches astride on the roof, and glares down at us. He breaks the tiles so that as soon as winter comes the neighbours remark: 'There's that Cottalus been at his old games again'.'"

Virgil evidences a specialist affection for battlements:

"Evado ad summi fastigia culminis, unde
Turrim in praecipiti stantem, etc., etc."

The eaves of farmhouses were Varro's choice:

"Habitat in columinibus villae."

The terrors of the smoky chimney in no way affected Martial's appreciation of the roofs:

"Me focus et nigros non indignantia fumos
Tecta juvant."

II. 90.

And he had formed a high opinion of their elevating effect:

"Puris leniter admoventur astris
Celsae culmina delicata villae†."

IV. 64.

An even higher estimate is that of Claudius Namatianus:

---

* Ausonius apparently suffered behind a careless leader of this type: "Illa meum petiit tegula missa caput." *Parent,* xi

† Yang I, the Chinese poet, echoes him: "Upon this tall pagoda's peak / My hand can nigh the stars enclose!"

"Non procul a caelo per tua templa sumus."

De Red. I. 5. 50.

It would have been matter for surprise had Juvenal in his universal fault-finding condoned by silence the over-ambition of the neophyte or the economic methods of the builder; yet it has been noticed in no commentary that he condemns them in a common moral:

> "Qui nimios optabat honores,
> Et nimias poscebat opes, numerosa parabat
> Excelsae turris tabulata: unde altior esset
> Casus et impulsae praeceps immane ruinae."
>
> *Sat* X. 105.

That among the Romans, indeed, the cult enjoyed a singular popularity*, being prosecuted even into the higher refinements of 'chimney-climbing,' Shakespeare is our authority:

> "Many a time and oft
> Have you climbed up to walls and battlements,
> To towers and windows, yea, to chimney tops,
> Your infants in your arms."
>
> *Julius Caesar* I. I.

Even in the general backwash of the Scholiast period, the vigour of the pursuit seems hardly to have diminished. The hungry swallows can find no more productive threat than that of destroying the finger-traverse of the door-jamb:

---

* The insult to a Wall in their eyes justified the killing of Remus.

"Εἰ μέν τι δώσεις, εἰ δὲ μή, οὐκ ἐάσομεν
Ἤ τὰν θύραν φέρωμες – ἤ τοὐπέρθυρον."

CELTIC

As a contrast to this Southern vigour, contemporary Celtic and Northern traditions offer few glimpses of an enlightened school. Ossian alludes to a posthumous ascent of doubtful authenticity: "It was the Wall of Thura, and the ghost of Cuchullin stalked thereon" (*Dar-thula*); but the Northern bards are content to enquire feebly: "To what end was wrought that roof ridge, the rings on the silver door" (*Nib. Lied.* Sig. i.).

ROMANCE

The spasmodic Romance literature bridging the chaos between the classic and our own is brightened by occasional flashes of intelligence. We find Charlemagne chaffing Alcuin for preferring the smoky roofs of Tours to the gilded fanes of Rome (*Epist.* 178); and similar to this is the delight of Sir Gawaine in *Sir Gawaine and the Green Knight* over "Walls set deep, that rose aloft to a wondrous height of hard hewn stone, adorned with fair carvings and turrets set in between with many a loophole: a better barbicane Sir Gawaine had never looked upon. And he beheld the tower... with carven Cornices, and Chimneys on the turreted roof, that looked fair to his eyes. And everywhere scattered on the battlements were to his eyes. And everywhere scattered on the battlements were Pinnacles... most pleasing were they!" but the result of his explorations is not given*.

Sir Tristram accomplished some remarkable wall-climbing feats against the Giants (see Whistlecraft, *Int, Nat. Work*, Cant. II.), and Sir Lancelot himself was a performer of no mean merit; it is pleasant to come upon him in a self-satisfied moment when, having apparently solved some awkward problem on the walls of Joyous Guard,

> "Above the gate, upon the tower
> Comely to the king he spake ...
> But have goodday, my lord the king,
> And you doughty knightes all;
> Wendeth home and leave your warring,
> Ye win no worship at this wall!"
>
> *Morte Arthur*

Queen Guinevere, it will be seen later, shared this taste.

After the age of Chivalry, internal discord and the growing MEDIAEVAL power of monasticism in the country seem to have produced a nervous reaction. Geoffrey of Monmouth assures us that "it required wonderful art to place the bones of Belinus at the top of the tower aforementioned" – now known as

---

* Similarly *Sir Guingamor* rhapsodises over "a great palace, well-built, yet without mortar (i.e. open-jointed)... Much it pleased him to see its beauties," etc., so much so that "merely to explore this house he lost all his labour" and forgot his Quest.

Billingsgate — and the Monk of Evesham, while tradition was too strong to allow him to exclude the wall from his 'Paradise,' yet represents the ascents thereon as of a most degenerate staircase nature:

"And also fro the gronde uppe to toppe of that walle were grycis (steps) ordened and dysposyd feyre and marvelusly, by the whyche the joyful company that was cum yn gladly ascended uppe. Ther was no labur, ther was no difficulte, ther was no taryng yn her ascendyng, and the hier they wente the gladder they were. Sothely y stode benethe on the gronde and long time y saw and behylde how they that cam yn ascendyd uppe. And some were seyne on the uppur partys of the walle as they had walkeyd hey thyr and deydyr."

Chap. 55.

The monks were in fact fonder of immuring than supermuring, and their baleful influence had its due effect.

If we except the 'larking' incident, naively and with not unnatural wonder recorded by James I of Scotland[*]:

"But for to se the sudayn weltering
Of that ilk quhele that sloppare was to hold,
It seemyt unto my wit a strange thing,
So mony I sawe that thun clymben wold
And failet foting, and to grownd were rold"

Kinges Quhair

---

[*] His descendant, James V., was the author of the good and godly motto, that should be engraved on every Climber's or Walker's heart or walking-stick: "Hearken what I say, *Grip ere thou slide* and *keep forth the high-way*" *Good and Godly Ballads*

we have to wait until Dante and Chaucer for an account of a definite incident or a description of a better state of contemporary proficiency. Dante is perpetually walking with "wary steps and slow, along the narrow verge" of some "battlement or cornice," or "clambering from pier to pier" of a bridge, but his detail is inferior to his English imitator, who may be taken as the more finished exponent of their age. Chaucer has been a literary benefactor to posterity in many ways. Not the least is an immortalisation of a fourteenth century ascent, which reveals a knowledge of the scientific rules of the art equal to any we possess at the present day; rules which cannot be better expressed than in his own words. In that climber's ideal, his House of Fame, "sixty myle of lengthe," even a "spoken word," we read, scorned a door and "went anoon up to a window out to goon" – "Or but hit mighte out ther pace, hit gan out crep at som crevace." Consequently we welcome without surprise and quote at length without apology the masterly description of Peter's feelings and performance on approaching the House, whither he has been dismissed by the Eagle "soom good to learnen in this place":

> "When I was fro this Eagle gone
> I gan beholde upon this place,
> And certein or I ferther pace
> I wol you al the shap devyse
> Of hous and syte –"

No Melchior could start more scientifically on his mountain, nor Ball more correctly on his guide book:

> "– and all the wyse
> How I gan to this place approche,
> That stood upon so high a roche,
> Higher stante there none in Spain."

He refers clearly to some previous exploration upon "Castles in Spain" or in the Pyrenees. Perhaps he followed, as co-explorer, the Royal route on the famous occasion, recounted by the fourteenth century rhyme, when

> "The King of France with twenty thousand men
> Climbed up the hill and then climbed down again;
> The King of Spain with twenty thousand more
> Climbed the same hill the French had climbed before."

Even De Saussure could not rival these expeditions in the matter of guides. We trust, however, our hero was present at the first ascent, in company with the lesser number:

> "Up I clomb with alle paine,
> And though to climb hit greved me,
> Yet I ententif was to see
> And for to pouren wonder lowe,
> If I could any weyen know
> What manner ston this roche was."

This is the true scientific and self-sacrificing spirit of the modern barometric climber:

"For hit was lyk a limed glas.

But that hit shoon ful more clere

But of what congeled matere

Hit was, I n'iste redely,

But at the last espyed I

And found that hit was everydele

A roche of yse and not of stele."

This passage is of great interest, illustrating the existence at that early date of the cross phraseology betwixt the mountain and the building*. Obviously the "congeled matere" spoken of by the writer as "yse" even as it would be in our modern technical tongue, is cement†. A conclusion made doubly-certain by the following lines expressing the contempt felt equally at the present day for this material and those who substitute its sham pretensions for real stone:

"By Saint Thomas of Kent

This were a feeble foundement

To builden on a place hye,

He oughte him litel glorifye

That him-on hilt, God so me save."

Yet even as now the Wilkins of the day had glorified himself by placing his name on the mouldings, and other climbers had followed the vulgar custom and scribbled their initials as

---

* Cp. Philemon Holland. "Anniball commanded his soldiers to stay upon a certain high hill, ... saying that even then they mounted the *walls' Passage of the Alps*

† See also Sir H. Wotton, p. 102

they passed:

> "Tho saw I al the hall y-grave
> With famous folkes names fele
> That had y-ben in mochel wele
> And hir fames wide y-blowe,
> But wel unnethes could I know
> Any lettres for to rede
> Hir names by, for out of drede
> They were almost off-thawed so."

Here we see that Peter knew his "sun-for-shade" rule, and was ascending his wall on the sunny side, where the cement had cracked and the mortar crumbled. We also learn that this rule was a comparatively recent discovery, for he proceeds:

> "I in my herte caste
> That they were molte away with hete,
> For on that *other* side, I seye,
> Of this hill that northward ley,
> How hit was writen ful of names
> Of folk that hadden grete fames
> Of olde tyme" –

the initials of famous climbers of the then old school, who had made shady ascents before the new law was acknowledged. Then Peter

> "Gan up the hill to goon
> And fond upon the coppe a woon (turret)
> That all the men that ben on lyve

> Ne han the conning to descryve
> The beautee of that ilke place.
>
> .   .   .
>
> It maketh al my witte to swinke
> On this castel to bethinke."

And he proceeds to rhapsodize on its beauties in a manner equal to any modern stegophilist, somewhat at first to our surprise, for we learn that the substance lauded was stone:

> "For why, methought, by Saint Geyle,
> Al was of stone of beryle
> Both the castel and the tour,
> And eke the halle, and every hour:
> Withouten peces or joinynges."

Here we detect the accent of disappointment to be looked for in the description of such a holdless material. But reassurance and the explanation of the previous praise follow at once in the joyful outburst:

> "*But!* many subtil compassinges,
> Babewines and pinacles.
> Imageries and tabernacles,
> I saw: and full eke of windowes
> As flakes fallen in grete snowes."

We need hardly explain that this phrase means that the windows came like welcome snow-patches on the cement ice-slopes:

> "And eke in ech of the pinacles
> Weren sondry habitacles (niches)."

But we will not intrude longer upon the privacy of these heart-revealing exultations, nor follow Peter's further roaming to

> "The castel gate on my right honde,
> Which that so wel corven was
> That never swich another n'as;"

where

> "Up he wente and that anoon."

Such mouth-aqueductive exultations are best left for private absorption.

During the Barons' Wars the art was put to too utilitarian a use to leave room for poetic record. In the innumerable stormings of castles, towns and churches, to get in was the only object, and the higher branches of method were lost sight of. The chroniclers, however, give us glimpses of the minuteness with which the practical side of the art was studied. Roger de Hovenden only admits "the architecture of a tower admirable" when it is "ornamented." Henry of Huntingdon can find no words strong enough to condemn Fitz Hubert, who captured Devizes Castle by a "new device of leather thongs thrown up the walls." The unknown author of the *Gesta Stephani* again and again attributes Stephen's failures to scale Exeter

Castle and others to the fact that they were "of hewn stone," and he is the authority for a statement that throws a startling illumination across this dark period, "that Stephen devoted large sums to Roofing"!

The next great revival seems to have taken place under the TUDOR PERIOD Tudors. Its effects are traceable not only in the literature but also in the architecture of the period. As will be apparent later, the alterations it induced in building fashions have left us houses unsurpassed for ascensional potentialities. On the literary side Ford, Gascoigne, Wither, Fletcher and Marlowe yield each their apposite allusions. Marlowe was also the earliest of our mural Germaniac school-reformers and wished to introduce the study of the science into the school curriculum:

> "I'll have them Wall all Germany with brass,
> I'll have them fill the public schools with skill."
>
> *Faust*

On a lower plane Barnaby Googe certifies the existence of a class of professional guide, apparently of no great merit:

> "Till at the length methought I might
> A Gorgyous Castell espy,
> Thear down began my guyd to fall
> And downward eake fell I."
>
> *Cupido Conquered*

Shakespeare reveals to us in the Sonnets how closely he

identified the roof with life, condemning interference with
those higher walks of life as practical suicide:

> "For thou art so consumed with murderous hate
> That 'gainst *thyself* thou stick'st not to conspire.
> Seeking that beauteous Roof to ruinate
> Which to repair should be thy chief desire."

Though he finds less to praise in the walls of the period:

> "The orchard walls are high and hard to climb,"
> *Romeo and Juliet*

and again:

> "The wall is high and yet I will leap down,
> Good ground be pitiful and hurt me not."
> *King John*

He erred on the same side of caution in the number of his
guides:

> "Return ... and fifty men dismissed?
> No, rather I abjure all roofs."

Recognising his own want of nerve, he resisted vainly the first
attacks of Climbing Fever:

> "*Hysterica passio*, down, thou climbing sorrow!"

And even called in the elements to remove temptation from
his way:

> "You cataracts and hurricanoes, spout,

> Till you have drenched our Steeples, drowned the Cocks."
> *King Lear*

Many evidences also of a cultured edificial taste are to be met with in Spenser. Witness the passages beginning

> "The turret's frame most admirable was"

and

> "The roof thereof was arched overhead,
> And decked with flowers and herbers daintily."

Great assistance these 'flowers' in truth! Indeed he relished this building much:

> "Ne can I tell, ne can I stay to tell
> This part's great workmanship and wondrous power.
> Which all this other world's work doth excel ....
> Therein were divers rows and divers stages,
> But three the chiefest and of greatest power,
> On which there dwelt three honourable sages.
> The wisest men I ween in all their ages!"
>
> *F. Q.*

Most sage old climbers! Spenser's applause is well deserved by their wisdom in selecting the strongest ledges as best suited to carry the weight of their advancing years.

With the income of the Stuarts and their attendant French influences a noticeable decline set in, and though the window and tree exploits of the two Kings Charles suggest that in its STUART PERIOD athletic expression the art was not entirely neglected, yet the decadent court Lyricists (with Marvell and J. Browne excepted) confined themselves to celebrating the mural powers of their ladies. Michael Drayton had foreshadowed this change, with his appreciation of an "ample roof" but dislike of the effort to reach it:

> "A rude and ample roof doth instantly begin
> To raise itself aloft, and whoso doth intend
> The length thereof to see, still going must ascend
> On mighty slippery stones."
>
> *Poly-Olbion* xxvi

And Pepys affords a typical example of the later general pusillanimity:

> "In Fleet Street received a great jostle from a man that had a mind to take the Wall, which I could not help!"
>
> (Feb. 1659.)

Again:

> "Much troubled this morning about the business of my walke on the Leads."
>
> (Oct. 1660.)

The Commonwealth brought with it the strong and healthy reaction which has not infrequently followed internal warfare and the accompanying storming of walled cities and castles. Among many it is sufficient to mention Milton and Cromwell as leading examples. Milton never grudged the time from his lofty poetical flights to visit exhilarating roof regions:

> "But let my due feet never fail
> To walk the studious cloisters'pale
> And love the high-embowed roof
> With antique pillars massy-proof;"

while of Cromwell we read that with characteristic mailed fist
and iron heel

> "Up the walls he clambered
> With nails most sharp and keen,
>   The prints whereof
>   On the board and roof
> Are yet for to be seen."

BUTLER, *Hudibras.*

But the demonstration died with the Restoration, and during
the long and dreary dominion of the Formalists which followed, muscular Naturalism hardly dared to show its head.
Chatterton forms a possible exception*: a single letter correction of Rossetti's spelling produces proof of the fact:

> "Thy nested home loves, noble Chatterton,
> The angel-trodden stair thy sole could trace
> Up Redcliff's spire."

But the mural ascent recounted by William Congreve in the
Mourning Bride, —

---

* pp. 85 and 109

> "The swarming populace spread every wall,
> And cling as if with clawes they did enforce
> Their hold through clifted stones,"

bears sign of internal exaggeration, and must probably be rejected as a serious narrative. If Pope and Dryden suffered for its suppression they only ventured to express themselves under the cover of translation*, yet it is not hard to read between the lines of Dryden's savage denunciation of the climbing of mountains:

> "Go, climb the rugged Alps, ambitious fool.
> To please the boys and prove a theme at school!"

MODERN
PERIOD

It was reserved for Goldsmith to inaugurate the new era of freedom, and, bold literary pioneer as he was, the liberality of his climbing propensities constitutes a yet more surprising feature in his somewhat timid personality:

> "Dear is that shed to which his soul conforms,
> And dear that hill which lifts him to the storms."
>
> *Traveller*

This is a breadth of view often lacking in the divided Wall and Hill Brotherhood, even at the present time.

Once started, and protected by Rousseau's philosophic advocacy of the worship of mountains, the subsequent history of orophism has been as progressive as a baluster descent.

---

* *Il.* and Ov. *Met. passim*

A great popular impulse was given at the end of the 18th century by the adhesion of Scott*,

> "who loved to crawl
> Up the low crag and ruined wall"
>
> *Marmion*

of Crabbe, who more placidly used to

> "Watch a wintry night on castle walls"
>
> *The Borough*

and of Wordsworth, who not only possessed all the climbing-poet's eye for a likely tower,

> "Watching with upward eye the tall tower grow
> And mount at every step, with living wiles
> Instinct"
>
> *Cathedrals*

but was himself a daring exponent of his theories, promptly

> "Flashing to that structure's topmost height."
>
> *Staffa*

Byron was ambitious, if occasionally characteristically indolent in his a-spirations:

> "Oh could le Sage's demon gift
> Be realised at my desire,

---

* He complains bitterly in his *Diary*: "We were not allowed to scale the steeple of St Geneviève" [1826], and elsewhere quotes from *The Revenge*: "I *like* the rocking of the battlements"!

> This night my trembling form he'd lift
> To place it on St Mary's Spire."
>
> *Granta*

Again, it is interesting to note that Keats' classicism prescribed his climbing no less than his poetic fields:

> "I escaped being blown over.... and the house being toppled on me; I have, since hearing of Brown's accident, an aversion to a dose of parapet and would rather have a harmless piece of Herculaneum than ever so modern a chimney-pot" (!)
>
> *Letters*

Shelley, of course, is a whole-hearted enthusiast* and, as has been noticed, no mean critic of style. Coleridge, to complete the great choir of Natural climbing bards, was a performer of promise rather than actuality. He erects a "pleasure dome" for his Kubla Khan, with what purpose is obvious, since

> "Twice five miles of measured ground
> With walls and towers were girdled round,"

but he terminates, to our regret, before he can get on to it.

PHILOSOPHIC SCHOOL

With the reign of the philosophic poets the art enters upon a less exuberant but increasingly scientific era. The part it has played in race evolution, its subjective effect upon its prosecutors, assume more and more the place of purely objective, picturesque descriptions.

---

* p. iv, and pp. 59, 113, etc.

Tennyson, often to be quoted, subjoins to the text of the Maiden Aunt on the need of "a universal culture for the crowd" the necessity of the earlier differentiation 'twixt those of whom

> "He had climbed across the spikes,
> And he had squeezed himself betwixt the bars."
>
> *Princess*

And Browning is almost opaquely emphatic on the educative influence:

> "Yon splintered mass amidst the solitude,
>   ...Nay; pour daylight in,
> The mound proves swarming with humanity ...
> Now you look nearer: mortal busy life
> First of all brought the crumblings down on pate;
>   ...What seems to you so picturesque
> To him is – but experiment yourself
> On how conducive to a happy home
> Will be the circumstance."
>
> *Turf and Towers*

The phases of Browning's development as a philosopher are so widely studied, that it is matter for surprise, and for correction, how little attention has been paid to the autobiographic sketch, given by the prophet and enshriner of this century's tectine progress, of his own *Sturm und Drang* period in the art. For his followers it is of considerable psychological value. Like many another he started, where no

> "friendly wit
> Knew and would teach him which was firm, which frail
> In his adventure to walk straight through life
> The partial ruin*; in such enterprise
> He straggled into rubbish."

The pathetically related downfall which followed set him searching for some dependable outside direction, and his quotation from a hitherto unidentifiable handbook indicates upon what worthless authority he elected to depend:

> "These steps ascend the labyrinthian stair,
> Whence darkling and on all fours out I stand
> Exalt and safe, and bid low earth adieu —
> For so instructs 'Advice to who would climb'
> And all at once the climbing landed him
> Where —"

Where such ascents on all fours by the back-stairs should land the misguided. His own experience induced considerable doubt, whether direction to others on his part was desirable. His conclusion with himself will be seen:

> "Do you advise a climber? Have respect
> To the poor head, with more or less of brains
> To spill, should breakage follow your advice!
> Headbreak to him will be heartbreak to you,
> For having preached 'Disturb no ruins here'
> ... a sage pedestrian picks his way!

------

* Cp. Shakspeare, Sonnet, p. 36

> What if there trip, in merry carelessness,
> And come to grief, a weak and foolish child?
> Be cautious how you counsel climbing then!"

But for those who share his passion and do not need his encouragement, he has a word of dearly bought advice:

> "Are you adventurous, and climb yourself?
> Plant the foot warily; accept a staff.
> Stamp only where you probe the standing point.
> Where you mistrust advance, stop short, there stick!
> Towers yet intact round turfy rottenness.
> Symbolical partial ravage, – keep in mind.'"

As a practical teacher his value is impaired for us, with our greater technical knowledge, by the error which originated his own mishaps – and led to his consequently somewhat fatalistic view, "Scale the roof of solid tops, and o'er the slope you slide!" – namely his extraordinary indifference to the relative suitabilities of materials:

> "Lead, lift at last your soul that walks the air
> Up to the house front, or its back perhaps;
> Whether façade or no, one coquetry
> Of coloured brick and carved stone. Stucco? well,
> The daintiness is cheery (!)."

Yet his philosophy of the art is profound, and he declares

---

* Cp. Richard of Cirencester, xxxvi. 4396: "A wall was made in an unskilful manner with more turf than stone, which was of no advantage *for their purpose*."

himself an unrivalled enthusiast:

> "I did go:
> ...climbed the ruined palace.
> Proved that the gate was practicable."

And again:

> "I could pass
> Life in a long midsummer's day
> My eyes from a wall not once away."

Well were it, could the general public be induced to lend ear to the final address of this our greatest exponent, on behalf of free progress:

> "Look at Baccheion's beauty opposite,
> The temple with the pillars at the porch;
> See you not something besides masonry?
> Well bear with the poor climber for love's sake!"

That this is no unneeded appeal an incident in a recent work of fiction is sufficient indication, when the heroine, simply as a matter of course, "fiercely tore off a handful of the climber from the pillar."*

ECLECTIC
SCHOOL

Matthew Arnold, a far less soulful philosopher of stones, represents for us the reactionary critical period following this creative eruption, and tending towards an eclecticism in climbing-edifices. He protests elegantly that only where

---

* *Heavenly Twins*

> "Far on its rocky knoll descried
> St Michael's Chapel cuts the sky,
> I climbed"

Carnac

a sentiment unconsciously imitated from the similar preference of the Chinese poet, T'sên T'san (760 A.D.):

> "A shrine whose eaves in far-off cloudland hide
> I mount."

Giles' Translations

Clough, as might be expected, is Classical in his preferences:

> "Alba thou findest me still and Alba thou findest me ever,
>   Now from the Capitol steps, now over Titus's Arch,
> Here from the large grassy spaces that spread from the
>   Lateran portal,
> Towering o'er aqueduct lines lost in perspective between,
> Or from a Vatican window, or bridge, or the high
>   Coliseum."

Amours

The number of his ascents is remarkable in so confined a
district. More recently Rossetti is found to complain of an
instance of philistinism –

> "It seemed a grip was laid on the walls
> To tug the house top down" –

so long ago as in James I of Scotland's captivity. He also
enquires:

> "Is there any roof that near at hand
> Might shelter yield to a hidden band?"
>
> *Rosemary*

This has been plausibly construed to mean a demand for a practice ground for the private efforts of the Pre-Raphaelite Brotherhood.

GERMAN
SCHOOL

Matthew Arnold again is our authority for the practice of the faith in an unexpected quarter of the second division of the recently connected Anglo-Saxon race:

> "Heine! Thou climbest again...
> To the stone-roofed hut, at the top."
>
> *Mar. and Paus.*

Among contemporary climbing German poets it may be noted incidentally that there is no passage more pregnant in the collected works of Goethe than his dignified recantation:

> "*Einst* war ich Freund von Narren,
> Wollte das Dach abtragen."

That his remorse was sincere there is evidence:

> "Das alte verfall'ne Gemäuer
> Durchklettre ich wie ich nur will."

He rates wall and hill as of equal value:

> "Und folge dam Zug
> Und Berg und Gemauer
> Umfittigen mir."

48

In the opinion of his elderly friends he subsequently carried his principles rather far:

> "Soll ich dir die Gegend zeigen?
> Muss du erst das Dach besteigen!"

Von Platen seems to have preferred night ascents:

> "Ohne zu schwindeln ergehn sie sich
> Mitten im Schlafe von Dach zu Dach."

And Schiller had a taste for turrets:

> "Er stand auf seines Dachas Zinnen."

His somewhat misfortunate experiences are referred to later[*].

The history of progress in France deserves more notice than it has been possible to bestow on it here. At the worst periods of English orophism, the art has never been known to suffer more than a temporary lapse on the gabled roofs of Paris, and through all the period of French hegemony, town tiles and Renaissance spires have been unceasingly crowded with the best boots in France. What say Henry of Navarre and his friends?

French School

> "Does Your Majesty fear an excursion on the roofs?'
> 'I am a chamois-hunter!'
> Getting out of the window la Mole clambered along the ridge and along by a gallery formed by two roofs."

---

[*] p. 92

49

Again:

> "He has escaped by the roof of the next house,' said
> Coconnas, putting his leg over the window-bar and
> preparing to follow on this slippery route. 'Bah! I am a
> mountaineer and used to traverse the glaciers.'"
>
> *Marg. de Val.*

It is remarkable that already in the 16th century the French had associated the two great Branches, and employed the interchangeable phraseology. A few years more and the technicalities are better understood: we find the Regent of France "embrassant la cheminé," "à califourchon sur le toit," and, with his companions, "descendant d'une rapidité sur la pente inclinée" (*Chev. d'Herm.*) – a veritable glissade, such as Cicero loved!

The escapades of the Duc de Beaufort at Vincennes and of Cardinal de Retz at Nantes are but samples of its popularity with the Fronde. The satirist Marigny performed a remarkable feat at Paris – "qui gagna le haut de la maison, en grimpant sur les tuiles."

Richelieu, Mazarin, and finally Dubois were all able performers in the same line: more modern instances are too numerous to find place here. French stegology may be summarised in the sentiments of its greatest poet:

> "Leap,
> Lover of antique turrets high...
> From fane to fortress, mount and fly

From belfry tall to frowning keep."

V. HUGO, *Waiting*

Among the members of the third Anglo-Saxon division these ethics of the brick-dust have been studied with characteristic fervour. There is a note of fresh exaggeration, significant of a new unjaded people, in Poe's flamboyant framing of his enthusiasm:

> "Up domes, up spires, up kingly halls,
> Up fanes, up Babylonlike walls.
> Up shadowy, long-forgotten bowers,
> Up sculptured ivy and stone flowers!"

City in the Sea

And Richard Dana's florid contempt for one who

> "builds no towering castles in the sky.
> Longing to climb,"

is scarcely less inspiring. Lacking this superficial efflorescence, Lowell's belief was probably yet deeper rooted. No matter what the sanctity of the occasion or place, his thoughts were never permitted to waver for a moment from the guiding principle:

> "In church, or palace, or judgment-hall.
> He marked great fissures that rent the wall."

Parable

And if, by ill fortune, the more conventional groundwork failed, he found perfect contentment

> "Climbing the loose-piled wall, that hems
> The road."
>
> *Beaver Brook*

"As the climbing, the character"; no less definitely than these lines accentuate the philosopher, or than Whitman's "My foothold is tenoned and mortised in *granite*" and his liking for gutters* evidence his unconventionality of view, the whole innocent self-confidence of the race stands typified before us in the characteristic Longfelonious verse:

> "Can others climb a balcony by moonlight
> As well as I?"
>
> *Victor*

THE LAST PHASE

Of contemporary literary record there is no call to speak further. We have the facts themselves before us. Whether future generations will succeed in compiling an adequate account of them from the watery extracts of our present minor poets remains uncertain. One drop of essence perhaps exists, in the quarter where force is usually awaited. Is a hope for the immortalisation of present climbing exploit or the last foothold of its degradation to be found in Rudyard Kipling's impressionist attachment

> "To the hush of the breathless morning,
> On the thin, tin, crackling roof"?†

---

* p. 95

† Characteristically Virgilian in sentiment as in phrase: "Tho saw I stand on a pillere, / That was of tinnèd iron clere, / The Latine poete Virgile." CHAUCER

CHAPTER THREE

WOMEN CLIMBERS

"Romantic maid!
Whether on nodding Towers you tread
Or climb the Andes' clifted side."

GRAINGER

No historical account could be complete without mention of the performances of lady roof-climbers. To many their existence may come as a surprise, and but for the recent spectacle of a lady scaling a five-storied hotel by the sun-shutters, its survival might even have been questioned here. This ignorance is partly attributable to the privacy to which dislike of being thought advanced has relegated its practice, partly to the self-absorption of masculine bards in their own achievements. In the primaeval cycle of wall-living, already described, teichology must have necessarily formed a branch of female education. The legendary Princess of the Golden Roof* must have earned the title from some ornate private roof-ground, similar

---

* German Folk Lore

to that of her royal contemporary "of the Glass Mountain," who, by the way, was the first climber to acknowledge the necessity of nails upon ice*. Documents make it clear to us that in the subsequent roof-ages there existed among the Hebrews the express regulation: "They shall run upon the wall, they shall climb up upon the houses, they shall enter in at the windows," and that this had its due effect is deducible from the fact that the recognised method of spreading gossip was to "proclaim it on the house tops." How absolutely universal the institution was among the early civilised Chinese, the remarkable simile employed by the poet Chang Chi is sufficient evidence:

> "Dusk comes: the east wind blows and birds
>> Pipe forth a mournful sound;
> Petals, *like Nymphs from balconies,*
>> Come tumbling to the ground."

Some remnants of the custom are traceable among the Greeks, though already privacy is an object. Andromache (in the absence of Hector), gathering her women about her,

> "ἔστη παπτήνασ' ἐπὶ τείχει"
>> *Il.* xxii. 463

and the sight of the somewhat forward Helen openly practising upon a tower causes considerable scandal among the

---

* German Folk Lore

Trojans*:

> "οἱ δ᾽ ὡς οὖν εἴδονθ᾽ Ἑλένην ἐπὶ πύργον ἰοῦσαν,
> ἦκα πρὸς ἀλλήλους ἔπεα πτερόεντ᾽ ἀγόρευον"
>
> *Il*, iii. 154.

Such prowess contrasts favourably with the decay among the later Greek ladies, which Heliodorus depicts for us:

> "τὴν δὲ Ἀρσάκην μὴ κατασχοῦσαν καθάλλεσθαι
> ἀπὸ τῶν τειχῶν."

While for the convention-bound Latin ladies the art had become practically non-existent, the super-woman Alecto, who to gain some private ends

> "Ardua tecta petit stabuli"
>
> *Aen.* VII

forming of course a divine exception. The only recorded expeditions were one of a tentative hysterical kind, not unknown at the present day:

> "Pavidae tectis matres ingentibus errant,
> Amplexaeque tenent postes!"
>
> *Aen.* V

and a second 'mixed' ascent, in which apparently nothing but the lady's deep affection could induce her to back up her lover on his ill-chosen masonry:

---

* It may be noted as our experience that the walls of Troy offer no peculiar difficulties to moderate climbers, with the single exception of the north bastion.

"nec saxo desiluisse time:
Ibimus, O Nymphe, monstrataque saxa petemus,
Sit procul insano victus amore timor!"

OVID, *Her*, XV. 174

A healthy revival illuminates the heroic age. Geoffrey of Monmouth is our authority for the fact that:

"The military men composed a kind of diversion on horseback, and the ladies placed themselves on the tops of the walls."

Chap. XIV

Similar prowess is recorded in the 14th century ballad of *Sir Triamour*:

"There was the fair lady set
Full heigh upon a turret."

In *Gareth and Lynette* there is evidence of a far more ambitious attempt:

" ...There was no gate like it under heaven
For barefoot on the keystone...
The Lady of the Lake stood...
... her great and goodly arms
Stretched under all the cornice... and over all
High on the top were those three Queens, the friends
Of Arthur; who should help him at his need..."

The Lady apparently needed no help; though we should like to know how she reached the keystone and whether the cornice proved too much for her. Rarely, however, is the recorder privileged to witness the performance:

> "Now *thrice* that morning Guinevere had climbed
> That giant tower … *till* she saw them come.
> And then descending met them at the gates."

In the 13th century the exploits of Saint Christina the Wonderful, the patron saint of our art, mark the culminating point of mediaeval teichophily. At the early age of thirteen she escaped from her own funeral procession and "swarming up a pillar perched upon the roof like a bird." The rest of her life was spent in scaling every attainable steeple, tower and gable, and her favourite attitude for meditation was "clasping a weathercock or vane."

The artificial position forced upon women by the gallantry of the Tudor and Stuart foplings led them to discard all secrecy, and their performances shine by contrast with their invertebrate adorers. We are inclined to assign to this date the exploits of the notorious Trochais*, and the old ballad of *Richard Coeur de Lion* relates of Cassodorien how

> "Out of the roof she gan her dight
> Openly before all their sight."

The Earl of Surrey, admitting his own feebleness,

> "When Windsor wall sustained my *wearied* arm,"

rhapsodises delicately over the

---

* p. 69

> "Sight of our dame
> To bait her eyes which kept the leads above."
>
> *Windsor Castle*

A similar tribute is that of Lord Buckhurst to his amorata:

> "Great was her force, whom stone walls could not stay!"
>
> *Mirror for Magistrates*

Probably to this date also must be referred the sudden descent euphemistically recorded by Byron:

> "From high Southarron's distant tower
> *Arrived* a young and noble dame[*]."

And to cite an instance of this feminine ascendancy from France, the fashion-plate of that age, we note that Voiture, the court poet, was decadent enough to pronounce it only

> "plaisant, que Mad[lle] de Rambouillet se promenant
> *sur la muraille* me reconneu *sur l'échelle*,"

and that la Grande Mademoiselle at a later date scaled the walls and captured the town of Orleans "on her own hands and feet."

Long inurement to suppression enabled the spirit to survive unchoked the dusty century so fatal to its male exposition. The only change effected seems to have been a relapse into conventional propriety. Opinion might hesitate to define the

---

[*] The moral is given by Henryson: "Her shoes should be of sickernesse / In sign that she not slide." *Garment of Good Ladies*

great Sarah as retiring, yet only when

"Marlbroke s'en va-t-en guerre,"

to the vast astonishment of the narrator does

"La dame à sa tour monte
(Mironton! mironton! mirontaine!),
La dame à sa tour monte,
Si haut qu'elle peut monter!"

Even the general enlightenment of the present century
has failed to remove these restraints, and the poets, for all
their realism, cannot give us anything resembling a connected
account of the progress. The isolated cases on record generally avail themselves of the cover of some subterfuge. Such is
Tennyson's:

"But as for her, she stayed at home,
And on the roof she went."

Shelley's Sister Anne-like lady was yet more bashful:

"With tombs and towers and fanes 'twas her delight
To wander in the shadow of the night."
Witch of Atlas

Only from America, if anywhere the home of the progressive woman, is an open ascent reported, even a failure
confessed! That the failure was not due to want of science
is evidenced by the employment of the Sun-for-shade Law,
indicated in the first line. Quite correctly the lady appears to

have made her attempt where

> "Summer assailed it from every side;
> But the churlish stones her assault defied,
> She could *not* scale the chilly wall."
>
> LOWELL, *Sir Launfal*

It is matter for hope that in our own land the enthusiasm may soon be more openly and universally displayed. At least one poetess has apparently discovered the royal road of the Pipes, which

> "Point me the excellent way which leads above...
> Up the high steep, across the golden sill"
>
> *Chr. Rossetti*

and Chimneys have also had their votaries:

> "About two years ago there was a woman climbed
> (chimneys) scores of times; and there is one at
> Paddington whose father taught her to climb."*

Who will deny that the inspired question,

> "How then a bride may keep your side when through a
>   castle gate you ride,
> Yet shall eschew the castle wall?"
>
> E. B. BROWNING

admits of but one rational answer? And the sex of its source indicates an awakening already begun.

---

* Sydney Smith, *Essays*

May not the increasing appreciation of mountain climbing abroad and house decoration at home significantly shadow a more general movement?

Possibly the season is not so far remote when the dull walls shall shine with a new presence, when the world shall see even

> "The kitchen malkin
> Clambering the walls"
>
> *Coriolanus*

and every lady climber may, as in Mr Swinburne's prophecy,

> "Now on the sheer city side
> Smile like a bride."*

Such in sketchy outline is the hitherto history of wall and roof effort. The preponderance of subjective impression over practical narration must be attributed to the literary abstractedness of its unconscious sources. Quotations in confirmation of detail might be multiplied without limit from the legend of Sanskrit origin anent the "House that Jack built," to Jack Sheppard's and Baron Trenck's escapades, or to Keats' "Fancied towers of delight ... rich opal domes, upheld by jasper pillars, letting through their shafts a blush of coral."†

---

* Cp. Tennyson's wish for all the Brotherhood: "...some comfortable bride to grace / Thy Climbing life."

† Keats conceived his ideal from the ascents in the *Passionate Man's Pilgrimage*: "Then the holy paths we'll travel... / *Ceilings* of diamond, sapphire floors, / High *walls* of coral." *An. Sc.* (1604).

But sufficient it is hoped has been given to indicate broadly the periods of blossom and decay, and the quarters where the richest finds may be made by those desiring to know further. References to specified passages will be gladly supplied, but students desiring a wider understanding on which to ground the structure of fict- or factional orophismic knowledge are recommended to neglect these chip-runnels and proceed at once to the original block-head. This may be found in the great anthology *"Walhalla, the Wallers Paradise of Song,"* which contains the body of scaling verse. Some additional works of value will be alluded to as occasion serves in the text and the names of a few rare volumes are appended, whose matter we should deem suitable for extended investigation.

CHAPTER FOUR

MATERIAL AND ARCHITECTURE

"Each clown may rise
And climb the skies
     When he hath found a stair;
But joy to him
That dares to climb,
     And hath no help but air."

WITHER, *Philarete*

A FEW words may not perhaps be out of place on the practical aspects of the subject, the age, material and style, best suited for experiment. The remarks must be necessarily general, as no definite rule can be made to fit the varying conditions, produced on the material by climate and by individual taste on style. Again, easy though it might appear to follow the example of the Climber's Guides and say, "these counties, Devonshire or Kent, or those towns, perhaps Chester or Hitchin, offer the best fields for exploration," yet, owing to the deplorable condition of society at the present day, which confines the householder exclusively to his own roof tree and, unfortunate paradox, prevents the public buildings laying open their exteriors equally with their interiors, such a course would be merely tantalising. Mention is only therefore made generally of the best type or date of architecture to be sought for by those who have opportunities of choice, and a few hints given as to the proper methods of dealing with them. Happy is the Englishman o'er whose brow rests an aged chimney pot or whose house is his castle. Most of us, alas, have to be content with practising on our castles in the air.

BUILDINGS Indubitably the buildings of monasteries, colleges or great schools offer the best training academies for those who desire to become masters of the art; and this for several reasons. They are as a rule collections of buildings erected at various dates and offering samples of every kind of architecture, all more or less joined together to form an irregular whole, fascinating as the "howling walls" of Caucasus itself to the enthusiast. Again, their economy of space offers easy means of access or retreat at any desired point through infinite attic windows, while their Gothic pretensions present many welcome hindrances, in the form of crenolated balustrades, to an undignified or unexpected descent of man. Since also the ownership of the buildings is vested in no one individual, it is nobody's interest to interfere with the climber and only the porter's business, whose mild but ever present terrors add just the sporting element lacking in ordinary Alpinism[*]. Consequently on the colleges, more especially those of Cambridge and Oxford, the art has always been prosecuted with the utmost enthusiasm from the earliest times. *The Merry Devil of Edmonton*

> "so many nights
> Watched on the top of Peterhouse' highest tower,"

and the Euphuistic Lyly found it necessary to protest against the Tudor undergraduates sacrificing all other studies to this one pursuit. "Learning," he suggested, "lieth neither in the freestones of the one (Oxford), nor in the fine streets of the other (Cambridge)." With the growth of more liberal views it is now possible even for strangers to live delirious days on these heights, or like Carroll's spook "shriek nightly on a battlement"; and no apology is necessary for taking our examples constantly from them.

Brick, stone, cement and iron, these are the principal wall materials, and stand here in order of their ascensional merit. MATERIAL

Brick is in truth the climber's joy, and properly used, as in former centuries, there exists no surer inoculator of the moenia-mania than BRICK

> "A stately palace built of squared brick

---

[*] *Teste* Ben Jonson: "So your stiffnecked Porter told me at the gate... which made me e'en climb over the wall." *The Lover Restored*

Which cunningly is without mortar laid
　　(i.e. open-jointed),
Whose walls are high but nothing strong or thick,
High-lifted up with many lofty towers
And goodly galleries far over-laid."

Faery Queen

Unfortunately it will be found that modern brickwork often falls far short of this true ideal, and a new wall nowadays with its uncompromising smoothness presents occasionally little less difficulty than the corner of a Fives Court –

"That Court, whose top to climb
Is certain falling, or so slippery that
The fear's as bad as falling."

Cymbeline

But kind Nature, who, as we mentioned above,

"cold and warm
And moist and dry, devising long,
Through many agents making strong,
Matures the individual form,"

is ever at hand to aid the climber, even though, as in the present case, she appear in the form of dishonest human nature. For modern mortar is generally shallow and always bad, and by means of a simple appliance attached to the toe somewhat resembling the tobogganing steering spike and a light pick hammer held in either hand, steps can be made up a fifteen foot wall (for preference a neighbour's) as successfully as with crampons and ice-axe up a similar ice slope. Charles Cotton commends a refinement upon this, covered nails fixed in the leather of the boot[*]: "the Second Way, which is done with Leather and Nails, is more proper ... but it cannot be made use of but upon Walls that are shot over with Plaister, for as much as otherwise your nails cannot hold," certainly an objection. His "Third Way, which is done with sheepshancks fastened in the Walls, is best and most commodious of all," but the driving of fixed iron spikes, though justified by the Matterhorn and hallowed by Tom Brown's and Harry East's immortal ascent of the School-House, partakes too much of the nature of artificiality to satisfy the hair-splitting of modern believers. Another method, which has the advantage of Marlowe's support:

> "I'll have you learn to sleep upon the ground,
> Sustain the scorching heat and freezing cold...
> And after this to scale a castle wall...
> For which the quinque-angle[†] form is meet,
> Because the corner there may fall more flat"
>
> *Tamb*, III. 2,

is to attack the wall corner, where it will usually be found

---

[*] *Planter's Manual*

[†] *Quinque*-angle possibly means a *Fives* Court (see p. 66). If so, an Eton one, where the "corner" difficulties are certainly simplified by the "flat fall" of the pepper-box

that the rotten mortar has crumbled out or can easily be per-
suaded to do so, leaving a possible though scrapey route to
the coping-col. If this be capped with bottle glass, a sack
or saddle may solve the difficulty, but such routes are best
treated at first with the respect they forced at the last even
from Pepita's lover*. In modern times the slovenly custom has
greatly increased of leaving brick ends projecting on house
corners as decorations or for future use. These will be found
to afford a delightful but precarious road to the slates; they
must be treated with great caution and care taken that the
weight of the climber be distributed evenly between his four
extremities, with the strain exerted as much as possible in a
transverse direction. Internal evidence tends to confirm the
warning tradition that it was the catastrophic consequences
of prosecuting his usual 'flashing' style over these untrustwor-
thy supports, which drew from the injured Wordsworth that
much-condemned expression of revengeful *Schadenfreude*:

> "Monastic domes, following *my* downward way,
> Untouched by due regret I marked *your* fall!"
>
> *Abbeys*

Ancient brickbuilding is however far pleasanter to deal with.
Of its earliest presentment the lonely towers of Nicaea or the
great walls of Constantinople afford an infinite variety of
sample problems, in their perfect brick rugosities; too perfect,

---

* "Pepita, Pepita, / I don't like that wall!" CORNEY GRAIN

alas, for the unhappy Greeks; as becomes apparent on finding
in the broken gaps,

> "Just where the ruinous walls they scaled"
>
> BYRON

courses of projecting tiles that must have offered all too ready
a foothold to the assailing Turk.

But the Elizabethan and early Stuart periods were its Golden
Age, and the world owes a greater debt to Christopher Wren
and Inigo Jones than it has yet acknowledged. Appropriateness
is beauty and Elizabethan houses confirm the saying, attractive
in their beauty of colour and shape and vastly appropriate for
climbing. Not a house but has its queer corners granting fric-
tional chimneys unequalled in the Dolomites, and its aimless fly-
ing brick-courses offering delicate traverses over the walls in all
directions, generously simplified by hand-holds in the decorative
brick-spaces; if ledges are lacking, the irregularly laid bricks with
their hollowed sides and deficient mortar supply their places,
while purposeless iron stanchions give excellent anchorage for
the rope on the cracked and bulging walls. The admirable chimney-stacks recurring at irregular intervals on the indiscriminate
gables, with their brick ledge traverses and indented 'corners,' bear
indisputable evidence of having been constructed for one purpose only, the convenience of the climber. There is little doubt
that one of these was the favourite problem of the enterprising
Trochais, celebrated by the "Anti-Jacobin":

> "Lo, where the chimney's sooty tube ascends,
> The fair Trochais from the 'corner' bends.
> Her coal black eyes upturned incessant mark
> The eddying smoke, quick flame and volant spark...
> Mark how his various parts together tend,
> Point to *one* purpose."
>
> *The Loves of the Triangles*

"Likewise the deep-set windows stained and traced" with their broad sills, or the frequent and still more grateful blind windows, make unrivalled resting places, and where chimneys fail firm water-pipes can be depended on to connect the whole system. Little recks — yes, very little wrecks — the climber as he crawls along some blind brick arch, steadied by a clothes-line from the attic-window, or wriggles up between the wastefully proximate chimney-stacks, that his efforts will probably end in smoke*. It is enough for him that "wrapt in his own imaginings" he mentally feels as if treading on air while he bodily feels that he isn't.

COSTUME, ETC.

For fuller particulars we refer to that excellent though somewhat decadent handbook, *"Brick-a-Break, or the Climbers Vadit Mecum,"* from which we may extract a few hints. In ascending brick chimneys, as on all stone-climbing, kletterschuhe,

---

* Cp. the chimney-climb in the *Wasps*: BA: οὗτος τίς εἶ σύ; ΦΙΛ: καπνὸς ἔγωγ᾽ ἐξέρχομαι. ARISTOPHANES. Other famous kapnodocists were the Taurians [Herod. iv. 103] and Mr Grimes, of Chimney No. 345 [*The Water-Babies*, Chap. viii.].

espadrilles, pampooties, scarpetti, apargates, tennis, or sand shoes are invariably worn, and Shakespeare recommends a snail-like gait*. The hair should be protected against the invasion of blacks by a close fitting cap, and a coat of khaki or mackintosh which will shift with less friction is found less agonising for the shoulders. The knees and joints should be leather-protected. The Rev. Sydney Smith, an expert in this branch, affirms that "in climbing a chimney, the great hold is by the knees and elbows," and he adds a word of caution for parents and guardians as to the helps necessary for beginners: "Above all, those who have chimneys accessible should encourage the use of machines†." In brick-traverses on the other hand strong-soled shoes give firmer hold, and a shuffling gait will be found less straining to the brick and trying to the balance. These brick ledges, often most useful in house-face climbing to connect window and pipe routes, are at once the most testing and interesting of all murine problems. They should not be attempted unless the climber be steadied by a rope from some window or stanchion, and even then the microscopic holds are a stiff trial of nerve and strength. Here alone is a hand-shake no friendly sign, and gladly often would the clinging finger-tips clutch at the straw foolishly rejected by Pharaoh from his brickmaking.

---

* "I'll *creep* up into the chimney." *Merry Wives*

† See Note p. 87.

STONE

Stone, it must be admitted, is inferior to brick as a climbing material. Whatever charm may be exerted on climbers in other lands by "the Imperial minarettes on high," in England:

> "The round squat turret, blind as the fool's heart,
> Built of brown stone, without a – [climbing] – part,"

cannot compete for charm with the variety and arrangement of native brick. The formation is widely different, but the difference is not for the better, and the word 'impossible' enters far too largely into its vocabulary. Its single advantage over brick lies in its reliability, and we confess that where the variety of brick and the security of stone are combined, as in the brick buildings of Emmanuel College, Cambridge, or the old mosque at Ephesus, where stone courses transect the old brick walls, a result is attained unrivalled in its transitory facilities and well deserving of the professed preference of the intrepid Cantab:

> "They dreamt not of a perishable home
> Who thus could build! Be mine in hour of fear
> Or grovelling thought to seek a refuge here."
>   WORDSWORTH

A full elaboration of the comparison, too lengthy to be treated of here, will be found in the exhaustive work entitled *"Stoneage and the Stonepagans"* with its sequel the *"Houseage and the Houseagents"*

Stone for the climber falls ordinarily into four heads: the
Classic, the Gothic, the Helpfully Decorated and perhaps his
own*. The first or Classic style is largely in evidence in our
public buildings and colleges, and we fear if Fifine were to
put to us the question "How does it strike you, this construction gaunt and grey, sole object these piled stones?" our
reply might be uncomplimentary; for the whole style is unequalled and combines the easy and the hopeless in a most
inartistic manner. Often on buildings strictly classical, such as
the British Museum, the University Library, the Louvre, the
Glyptothek at Munich, or the great marble theatre at Miletus,
do we groan with despair over a series of grand three-foot
courses running directly one above the other, but connected
only by impassable faces. The Classic architect had no eye
for placing a pipe, and his Doric columns are widely spaced
and possible only for an Atlas to shin up. Spenser, it is true,
rhapsodizes on a bridge that

> "y-built in goodly wize
> And arched all with porches did arize
> On stately pillars framed after Doric guize,"

but it has been pointed out that his pleasure is clearly due
to finding its difficulties simplified by "curious corbes and
pendants graven faire," and as a general rule the aggravated
climber could

---

* "I must ere long lie as lowly as they / ... with a stone at my head." W. COWPER

> "From every building, gay or solemn,
> Well spare the shapely Grecian column."
>
> CLOUGH

But as it is he must put his pride in his (outside) pocket and be content to be lowered from the window to the abused ledges. (For methods of suspension see *"Window-pains or a Silly Start"* by *Beginner.*) Once there he will find that, however narrow they may look from below, they are usually wide enough to afford rare opportunities for a bicycle-track and rarer ones, let us hope, for a rescue by the garden ladder. Virgil, as we know, had a classic affection for such routes:

> "Vergilio mi venia da quella banda
> della cornice, onde cader si puote
> perchè da nulla sponda s'inghirlanda"
>
> *Purg*, XIII

but we also know him to have been amateurishly indiscriminate in his use of buttress or ladder[*]:

> "We reached the summit of the scale, and stood
> Upon the second buttress ... a cornice there," etc.

and his opinion carries little technical weight.

Occasionally of course the ledges *may* prove too narrow to turn upon, and here a rope slung from window to window makes a reassuring handrail. In any case they are always in

---

[*] Cp. also Caesar *de B.G.* 5.43, and *B.C.* I. 48

themselves secure and offer no excuse for stumblers; if a trip-per chance to fall – on his own head be it!

In stone however, as in brick, the Golden Age has come to our assistance and set an example of ideal Classic architecture which has fortunately found many later imitators. Observe for instance the older buildings at Holy rood, or still better the Trinity Library, Cambridge*. Crowned though it be with four blank and impossible 'faces,' it is yet not more attractive to the eye than it is agreeable to the hand and foot. A mixture, as the guide-books inform us, of the Doric and Ionic styles, the junc-tion has been marked by a gratifying wealth of excrescence, and the kindly Wren had clearly an eye throughout to the needs of the climbing brood. The columns (Ionic) are placed 'grandly contagious' (Native Doric) for chimney purposes, and

> "Round the roofs a gilded gallery
> That lends broad verge to distant lands"

in the form of a broad terrace or "Rake's Progress" crosses the face from end to end. Noble waterpipes set back in roomy chimneys connect this with the ground, and higher a variety of routes up pipes or along blind windows, stone courses and hanging garlands lead to the final balustrade. Heartily do we

---

* Evidently built after Francis Bacon's recipe for a climbing edifice: "I would have it two stories, of eighteen foot high; and goodly leads upon the top, railed, with statues interposed with embellishments ... not a naked wall, but enclosed with terraces leaded aloft, and cloistered with pillars ... with some low galleries to pass from them to the palace itself."

commend this style to the attention of builders. It is an excellent improvement upon the crude outlines of the Parthenon and if it but become more generally popular the mastering of Classic architecture will be a less hopeless study for the Modern School of climbers*.

Gothic architecture to most minds suggests the Gothic interior of a Church; but climbers do not find this connection so inevitable, since for obvious reasons the holders of the true faith are rarely able to make trial of this or any other style in its ecclesiastical presentment. Shakespeare of course is a climber before everything, even in church:

> "should I go to church
> And see the holy edifice of stone
> And not bethink me of the dangerous rock?"
>
> *Merchant of Venice*

but he is to be regarded as an exception, and no long description would be necessary or becoming. It may be understood that the few observations here given were collected during the process of church decoration and are intended only to be used as aids to the same. Many authorities indeed now wisely advocate the view that

---

* The Parthenon and the Theseion have defeated all our efforts, but the ancient builders may be less responsible for the present inutility of their structures than the decline in the human climbing powers. Poe, alluding to this very Parthenon, speaks of a time when positively "*Beauty* clung around her columned walls." *Al Araaf*. The Erechtheion has proved less stubborn.

"Church ladders are not always mounted best
By learned clerks"

COWPER

and co-opt lay experts. Though in estimating clerical claims
in this line Jonathan Swift's and de Quincey's evidence must
not pass unheeded; Swift notes

"A traveller who by did pass
Observed the Roof amid the grass,
On tiptoe stood and raised his snout
And saw the parson creeping out."

It is no surprise to read further of this stegophilistic divine
that

"The neighbouring farmer calls
The steeple, Knocks*, the vicar, Walls."

De Quincey recounts a remarkable church scene:

"Every pinnacle of the fretwork, every statue of
advantage amongst the traceries, was crested by
white-robed choristers."

But these performances seem to have called for comment as
exceptional even in their own age.

Ruined abbeys and churches are of course permissible
ground, and as most of the remarks will apply equally to
them, "the blackened arches of fair Melrose" may be taken by

---

* See p. 80

nice-minded readers as their mental picture throughout*.

ROMANCE

In the first place all Norman and Roman stone architecture can be at once rejected. One of the most eminent experts has not hesitated to express his condemnation of them in the irritated apostrophe:

> "Stay then, stoop, for I *cannot* climb
> Yon great shapes of the antique time."
> BROWNING

And the estimate is just. The round Norman arch with its plain chamfers and shallow roll-and-hollow, the heavy column with its blunt fillet and simple capital give little satisfaction even in a ruin; for so firmly is the stone laid that even in decay it will no more yield one inch to the foot of man than twelve to the yard-dog.

TRANSITION

Transition is devoid of special interest, though the heavily-carved granite exteriors of some of the Cornish churches, such as Launceston, lend it a specious attractiveness. And it is only when we come to Early English that we find anything

EARLY
ENGLISH

worth real attention. Stone-cutting appears here as a real art, and the satisfactory result of the long struggle between the

---

* Melrose, Furness, Fountains and Glastonbury Abbeys offer several interesting minor window problems: in Haddington, on the ruined church tower, there is still a stick erected as a challenge by a boy early in the 19th century, and unrecovered. County Kildare, and in fact Ireland generally, is full of ruined churches of considerable merit.

climbing and non-climbing members of the Architect fraternity, of which the only record survives in the lines:

> "And we came in an evil time to the isle of the
>   Double Towers,
> One was of smooth-cut stone, one carved all over
>   with flowers,
> Till the passion of battles was on us, and all took sides
>   with the Towers;
> There were some for the clean-cut stone, there were most
>   for the carven flowers"
>
> *Voyage of Maeldune*

begins clearly to evidence itself. The deep-scooped hollows
with the large-swelling roll give a grand grip; the door pilas-
ters are not mere semicircles carved on the corner-stone but
separate pillars shyly-welcoming a friendly hand-clasp, while
in the highly moulded bases and on the stiff-leafed ornamentation of the capitals a plethora of hand-hold will be found;
hold which becomes a perfect hurricane-deck when the grasp
encounters the ideal 'cushion-mouldings' unrivalled even by
the Parson's Nose (on Snowdon) for suspensional convenience. Gothic arches are of course imitated from mountain
forms, and though it is never possible to scale the interior of
a peak, yet the 'back and toe' ascent up the inside of a narrow
door-arch or lancet and the breath-holding reach out at the
summit for the edge of the ruined wall or, in the aforementioned co-opted circumstances, for the ledge of the cornice

or clerestory, demand a balance rarely credited even to the most famous mount-a-banks; even Byron's acrobatic moon thinks twice before tackling such a problem on its ascent[*].

The steeple is by nature the culminating point of this popular style. The *Humorous Lieutenant*, in an earlier age, contemptuously remarks:

> "He does not follow us!
> Give *me* a steeple-top!"
>
> FLETCHER[†]

and it seems to have been popular with the Cavaliers as contrasted with the Roundheads:

> "They in their squeaking laugh contemn
> Us, as we walk more low than them,
> And from the precipices tall
> Of the green Spires to us do call."
>
> AND. MARVELL

Whether it be attempted on Byron's ladders or Chatterton's soul, on the open stone-work of Strasbourg or the Steeple Jack's ropes, with the painful failure of the cynical Neighbouring Farmer[‡] or the blatant triumph of Mr Kipling's

---

[*] "But when the rising moon begins to climb / The topmost arch, it gently pauses there!"

[†] Cp. Sir W. Scott's enthusiasm, p. 41, Note.

[‡] p. 77, who "calls the steeple, Knocks!"

Purple Emperor*, all authorities agree that the sensation is stimulating and that it is not wise to sit astride of the vane on reaching the summit, unless endowed with the abnormal nerves of our great patroness Saint Christina the Wonderful.

It is the more to be regretted that the British hold very few steepling records. The distinguished teichophilist, Sir Francis Vere, secured a few first ascents by proxy:

> "Sent up to the top of the steeple
> Sir W. Constable and other gentlemen"
>
> *Commentaries*

but it is an Italian who lights the bonfires on the curved dome of St Peter's on the Pope's accession; the hunchback immortalised on the summit of Notre Dame was a Frenchman; an Austrian ran round the cornice of the Innsbruck belfry tower, and even in our own country and in the golden days of the Tudors, Underbill informs us that:

> "Before Queen Mary's time I beheld Paul's steeple...
> and a man Peter, a *Dutchman*, triumphing and dancing on
> the top." (1562)

This surely calls for correction.

Beginners may obtain good practice on the Hall pinnacles of Trinity College, Cambridge, and the Gothic fountains at Nuremberg, Smyrna, Oxford, Budapesth and Hyde Park

---

* "She climb up der Shteeple, / Und she frighten all der people, / Singin' michnai – ghignai – shtingal – Yah!" '007

(close to the gate into the Bayswater road). For more advanced climbers the spires of Milan and Cologne Cathedrals, the minarets of the Green Mosques at Brûsa and Nicaea and the pinnacles of the Houses of Parliament – accessible by broad ledges from the Colonial Secretary's window and by a very stiff chimney-climb from the Terrace itself – afford an excellent introduction to this class of aspiring ascent.

SECULAR
GOTHIC

Secular Gothic in its various stages is a common enough style in College or Town architecture. It lacks the wreathed column and the ribbed arch and is popularly reckoned below the ecclesiastical article in elevational value. It has however some advantages over the Chancel style; the use, for instance, of the blind arch (for the origin of which refer to the treatise on *"Walleye or Stoneblind"*); again of the buttress, probably the "easy way up" contrived by early Wallites for their children, which is now largely used for ornamental purposes and may be readily made to serve useful ones. The windows also are commonly surmounted by ledges, which, if the storeys be not high, remove the necessity of a staircase; and the roof edges are bountifully blessed with the aforementioned giddy turrets and swaying stone spires similar to those on St George's Chapel or Milan Cathedral, a form of exhilarating wayside problem which excited Tennyson's enthusiasm as almost too good to be true – so we learn at least from his exclamation on buildings "pricked with *incredible* pinnacles into heaven."[*]

Cement or concrete, so often used to imitate Gothic stone
formations, may be fittingly introduced under this heading.
It has been customary with roof tourists to abuse architects
who produced specious efforts with a material fair seem-
ing but rotten at the core. But climbers are compassionate
to the architect and give thanks for his work. They are tired
of the so-called free-stone walls, in reality firm as iron, and
they desire a free-masonry with a less elusive grip. To them
the crumbling heights are rotten peaks and risky ice-slopes
calling for caution, judgement and skill, and granting many
opportunities for a literal, though perhaps painful, cementing
of friendships. The skill and judgement may not be at once
attainable, but the caution should be sedulously emulated by
all who attempt such places, for by this alone can the griev-
ous results which led to the unfortunate "Scholar's Funeral"
be avoided:

> "Down he falls
> Upon the pavement with a shuddering groan.
> Then dumb he lies, and ever and anon
> Fixes his eyeballs with a ghastly glow

---

[*] Numerous ascents on Castles and Fortresses, such as Karytana, Rhodes,
Chios, Carisbrooke, the Castles of Wales and of the valleys of the Rhine,
Loire and Danube might be cited, but as the products of decay, earthquake or
assault they do not admit of classification as a Style or Period. Modern stone
buildings are made of cement or imitate its forms.

On the damp blackness of that hideous 'stone.'"
WILSON

Much experience can be gained on the numerous early Victorian "castles" – in Ireland called Follies – erected by large landowners after this model. A gratuity to the caretaker covers objective damage. To guard against subjective injury one need only remember that no hold however firm should be singly relied on, no pinnacle however large be trusted as rope anchorage; flower and window mouldings clatter at a touch and a whole battlement has been known to snap off in the grasp of an eager leader and precipitate him and his companions in a concrete jumble into the gutter:

> "'Yon buttress still can back me up,' he judged,
> And at a touch down came both he and it."
> *Turf and Towers*

The delicate corner-turrets so fascinating alike to the vitiated expert and the expert novice are mere men-traps, constructed on the principles of an Indian mud-gaol to crumble at sight. The panting climber as he slowly kicks steps up the peeling plaster finds himself frantically holding the trembling masses together in his embrace, and when Laon-like, the crater won, "he stands upon the point of shattered stone, and hears loose stones rushing tumultuously," and perhaps loose language doing likewise – he recognises, and truly, that he will be lucky if he gets down without the whole tottering erection "dropping like the gentle rain from heaven" in his company*.

The third great division of stone, which we called the Help- fully Decorated, is at once impossible to fully describe because of its complexity and unnecessary because of its simplicity. All honour to Inigo Jones, who outdid even the amiable Wren and his school in the greatness of the benefit he bestowed by popularising Italian architecture. He has left us monuments of himself in buildings such as Clare College, Cambridge, which "shall be the record of the builder's fame for aye." This latter especially presents all the perfections of his commendable style; the set-back storeys, the short pillars, the frequent ledges with first-class anchorage in desainted niches, and above all the indented corners†. As the climber gazes up at these delights the Spirit of Bythryck gurgles perforce in his throat:

> "What wondrous monument, what pile is this,
> That binds in wonder's chain entendement.
> That doth aloft the airy skyen kiss
> And seemeth mountains joined by cement?"
>
> CHATTERTON

---

* Note the experience of *Sir Libeaus Desconus*: "Seeking for one to fight, he searched on the 'corners' and over the 'strange pillars': the stones from out the wall fell on him!"

† Ben Jonson alludes to his experiences here in a pregnant passage: "These porticoes were builded, seats for knights / That watched for all adventures, days and nights, / The niches filled with statues, – to invite / Young Valours forth!" *Prince Henry's Barriers*

The porter may reply "Clare College, sir, and you'd best go home straight," but the swift-rolling eye of the climber passes crushingly over him as it runs rapturously aloft on an ideal journey that the body would fain follow:

> "And when he came on carved monuments,
> Spiring colosses and high raised rents,
> He past them over quick as the eastern wind."
>
> BROWNE, *Britt. Past*

Indeed the collective merits are too numerous for recital; but the corner moulding just mentioned, which follows somewhat the principle of the projecting brick-bat*, deserves special notice, as its introduction in spite of some growing faults has done much to improve modern stone-climbing. In old buildings indeed the "'twixt and 'twixt" divisions were deep and sharp enough to make ascent easy, though we question whether the verse assigned to a 17th century don,

> "Full lightly would I up,
> With handes and feetes bound,"

has not a comma too many for probability. But in modern imitations the moulding divisions are apt sometimes to be uncomfortably obtuse-angled, and on occasions a mechanical

---

* See p. 68

contrivance*, somewhat like a curved fly's foot or the dart of an air pistol, projecting a few inches from the chest, may be found useful, not as a support but as an aid to retaining the balance while the hand is reaching for hold. This convenient instrument is called a 'scoop,' probably from 'stethoscope'; it cannot be charged with more artificiality than a boot-nail and need only be used in emergencies; when such present themselves the hanger-on has but to

> "Set his bent bow to his briest
> And lightly lep the wa'."

Renaissance ornamentation for our purpose is but qualified Gothic, and as the more various the adornment the easier the climbing, the less said about it here the better. In a ruined refectory window it may serve a useful purpose, and undoubtedly unremarked fountains† or impossible porches are rendered problems worthy of attention by its means‡. Latterly on the Continent such baroque or rococo assistance has had a certain vogue, more especially on public buildings and

---

* Probably the "ascendens machina" of Vitruvius, 10. 13 (19) 3. It is to be distinguished carefully from the 'truncheon' invented by Kingsley to help *Tom* up "the enormous wall, which seemed ninety feet high," and which "sent him up to the roof in no time." This was applied in a different manner.

† "Fountain *heads* and pathless groves, / Places which pale passion loves."
J. FLETCHER

‡ To those already cited may be added the "sprawler" fountain in Vienna, Paris and Munich *passim*, and innumerable British Jubilorials. The Martyrs' Memorial at Oxford has a recorded ascent only as far as Cranmer's head.

railway stations. Some superficial trials however at Cologne, Bucharest, Vienna (Nord-West) and Athens were not reassuring as to its security, and Shelley appears to have made the same observation:

"Not all to that bright Station dared to climb,"

though this last has been referred by some to St Pancras and by others to Blackfriars Bridge. Similarly the delicate marble tracery that appears to simplify many a Persian mosque porch and minaret, as it does many Grecian and Egyptian bas-reliefs, is rarely of sufficient depth to give foot-hold to any but the heaviest nailed boots. But apart from questions of safety the fretted stone-work conveys a bald impression of artificiality, unpleasing to the Simon-like simplicity of petrophilists. Let no one cry out upon this as hypercritical hair-drawing; as we have endeavoured previously to show, all building is governed by the laws of mountain architecture and the murine mind rejects as artificial anything that has not its colline counterpart. Firmly therefore but with all modesty we protest against these blessings in disguise, and assert a preference for our peaks in a state of nature. The same objection applies to most Victorian, Byzantine or other-ine stonework; such at least is the impression produced by a scrapey examination of the Alhambra, Imperial Institute and Albert Memorial. But it would be presumptuous to pass a final opinion before some such edifice has been especially devoted to the gaining of a practical knowledge.

Flint is probably the most disappointing of all structural materials. No doubt if the climber be lucky enough to come
upon some old flint wall, say of two centuries ago, with its
large masses sufficiently ruined for holding purposes but not
often enough climbed to have become dangerous, he may obtain two or three fine arête scrambles upon it. Some of the
old belfry towers, more especially in the north, offer magnificent perpendicular corners of this kind. No doubt Mr Austin
Dobson had some such route in mind in asking:

> "Who tolls the bell once more?
> He must have climbed the parapet;
> Did I not bar the belfry door?"
>
> *Belfry*

Where also brick is combined with flint, toe-scrape ascents
by the rude joinings are often feasible, and we know of a certain summer house constructed on this principle which though
only thirty feet in circumference has been ascended by no less
than ten stone and six ivy routes of varying sensationalism and
difficulty. But Flint by itself is a structural failure and would
serve as an admirable copybook example of the inexpediency
of placing jewellery around the necks of Greek statues. The
uninitiated would doubtless imagine that by piling rough flints
loosely together into a wall — Cato's pet 'maceria sine calce ex
caementis et silice' (*R.R.* 15) — the nearest possible resemblance
to a mountain has been obtained. But old wine finds proverbi-
ally a scanty following in new bottles and the flint when massed

into a wall gains none of the advantages of systematized brick or stone and retains few of its merits as rock. The regulation wall-chinks are all eliminated, for the rough-shaped stones are fitted corner-wise into one another or the mortar, instead of being laid overlappingly upon it, and we have nothing left but painfully sharp 'one finger and scrape' holds placed at impossible distances. "Flint were an ugly devil," cried a third pirate with a shudder, "that blue in the face too." "That was how the rum took him," added Merry; "blue, well I reckon he was blue."* And the climber as he gazes desperately up at the speckled blue face of some East Anglian church tower and feels the caerulean tint creeping into his own, mentally confirms the words of the third pirate and turns sad and unsatisfied away, wondering how the saints the rum *did* take it!

WOOD

Wood is but meagrely represented in our own country in large structures. In its plank formation it is to be found in country barns and sheds, but by a singular contrariness with all the holds turned downwards. Rustic summerhouses are possible scrambles, but scratchy, frail and generally stickily varnished. They find favour however with Robert Bridges:

> "High on the mound the rustic arbour stood,
> A dome of straw upheld on rustic wood;
> ... unto the southern front we went,

---

* *Treasure Island.* It is lamentable that Stevenson "found no interest in a string course except for purposes of romance"! but possibly "romance" has a secondary meaning; see p. 116, App. A.

And from the dark plantation climbing," etc.

New Poems

The temporary pole formations of scaffoldings or hoard-ings rarely come up to expectation. The slopes and intervals are too uniform to allow of variety of treatment, and leg-swarms and arm-pulls in regular sequence become monotonous even at a considerable height. As helpful, if fragile, assistance in the form of trellis-work or conservatory buttresses, its merits must be conceded on occasions, and the beams or rafters of old Cheshire houses or large halls can be used as sensational 'hand' or 'chin' traverses. One of the earliest experts in this line appears to have been one "Vary of Draws," of whom the *Mabinogion* records that he

"Spread his red, untrimmed beard over the eight and forty Rafters which were in Arthur's hall"

Kilwych and Olwen

and Barnaby Googe's friends found them useful in emergen-cies:

"some downward fall
From Houses hye by heapes,
Some Anker cast on crossed Beames."

*Cupido Conquered**

---

* A recent rafter-ascent by a vigorous lady calls for some notice: "But now / Shakes she the ringing Rafter ... with festal footing." FRANCIS THOMPSON *New Poems*

PLASTER   Excursions upon the variety of lath and plaster come too near incurring the accusation of unjustifiable risk to be recommended in a standard work of this class. But to avoid misconception it may be accepted that if the partition be held by a strong wall paper an expert climber can, by careful step-kicking, avoid the usual catastrophe at the ceiling; but he will rarely – for several reasons – be allowed to return upon his steps. All recorded attempts either on roof, ceiling or party-wall have ended alike. Of the ceiling Schiller could hardly find words strong enough to express his feelings:

> "Sei grimmig mir gegrüsst, feindselig Dach!
> Verhasstes Pflaster!"

and with more self-restraint Pliny records simply of the partition:

> "perfodivi parietem in eo conclavi."
>
> *Mil*, 2. I.

On modern imitation Cheshire houses a precarious exterior ascent can be made by kicking steps in the rough-cast just above the sham wooden cross-beams and getting 'side-pull' finger-holds between the uprights, but these attempts are not advised.

IRON   Iron was the last of the materials on our list, and is included here rather on account of the importance it may attain to in the future than of any great climbing value it possesses at present. More and more every year is iron being employed in large erections, witness the new Tower Bridge, and some day of a surety it will have to be seriously reckoned with by climbers. But at the present time few of the modern existing examples are available for private practice and the ancient "sword into ploughshare beaters" were too sparing of their material or chary of depreciating their coinage to leave us an iron monument or even a metal base*. It is true that we have in the authentic Rowley poems record of a somewhat remarkable building:

> "Stay, curious traveller, and pass not by
> Until this feetive pile astound thine eye,
> Whole rocks on rocks with iron joined survey,
> And oaks with oaks commingled ordered lie."

'Feetive' is an expressive word that calls out for adoption by climbers, and we should recommend the whole pile as a handy model for a millionaire desirous of an improved iron-bound Matterhorn in his back yard. But the metal in it plays a subordinate part (we cannot even tell whether it was cast or beaten) and we have to fall back upon the Eiffel Tower as the only iron worthy at present to enter the climber's sole. The French have always had a predilection for this material: Louis XI "enclosed his Castle of Plessis with a grate of iron," and "caused four strong towers of iron to be built at the corners,"

---

* Chaucer in the *House of Fame* records the ascent of an iron pillar by Homer, Statius and Lucan, of a lead column by Josephus and of a copper ditto by Ovid. Times and details are lacking.

on which he was wont "to take his exercise."* The distinctive feature of ironing lies in its open lattice-work, at once so oppressive to the nerves and grateful to the hand, and Eiffel's Tower is worthy to rank with Swift's 'Tub' as a monument of this style, combining in perfection the apparent openness and actual opposition which give irony its peculiar charm. Such being the case it is indeed regrettable that it is only possible to state here as the result of eye examination that the crossed girders should give magnificent climbing, certainly so far as the projecting first stage, possibly to the last. Unfortunately a praiseworthy attempt to amass first-foot knowledge by crossing the great arch-span was perfidiously frustrated by the *gendarmes*, who appeared to regard the proceeding as a secret method of smuggling dynamite to the summit and an insult to the fighting metal of their army[†].

WATER PIPES   Water and gutter pipes do not rank perhaps scientifically as iron, but gratitude for their frequent succour in distress urges the piper to raise to this dignity at least pain-killers so often worth more than their weight in gold to him. Popular

---

[*] Danett. Louis was also an advocate of fixed spikes: "He caused to be masoned into the wall a great number of iron spears, their heads set close together" *Ibidem.* His monotonous "grate of iron" reveals an equally jaded climbing taste.

[†] For beginners the vast metal statue of Cardinal Borromeo on Lago Maggiore offers good outside scrambling on the drapery and, inside, a moderate climb to the height of the nostril. The "Copper Horse" in Windsor Park makes an excellent elementary problem, as also the statue of Frederick the Great in Berlin, first ascended by a boy, Fritz Muller, on the receipt of the news of Sedan.

opinions can afford to be neglected when tried friends are in question, and pipes are so little accustomed to stand alone that it is only justice to attach them here to some firm material. Walt Whitman, it should be noticed in passing, had a particular affection for these "slender high roads":

> "Over the sharp-peaked farmhouse...
> With the slender Shoots from the Gutter...
> I tread day and night such roads."
>
> *Of Myself*

Pipes proper are of two classes, the round and the square. But they are as infinite as the unclassifiable water-gully in their cunning. If the concave gully threatens with a loose interior, following the law of parallels the convex pipe overwhelms with a rickety exterior. If the gushing gully-pitches weep damply into the peck of the pitcher, the leaky pipe-joinings convert the joiner into a subsidiary water course. If the rottenness and the wriggle-compelling straightness of the gully has earned for its admirers the insulting title of 'Chimney sweeps,' equally so has the embrace-enforcing steepness of the pipe won for its devotees the unenviable soubriquet of 'Pipe-cleaners.' The domestic aqueduct may be in short inferior in variety to its gullian anti-type, but it is its equal in the severity of its difficulties and surpasses it in its absence of all lateral escape.

The Elizabethan age was famous for many beneficent inventions; some have been previously noted; some, such as the exploiting of tobacco or the exaltation of the lyre, are only indirectly connected with pipes proper, but of the remainder none can compare with the perfecting of the Gutter-Pipe. Let but the wall be of Tudor or Jacobean brick and whatever the apparent inaccessibility the assailant can afford to make light of it, confident that in some corner stands the betraying skeleton, a rough gritty pipe set some three inches from a foot-caressing wall, gripped at its every joint by a broad collar and clamped by fastenings to its family Caucasus, immovable as Prometheus. Even on such secure ground however some caution is necessary in passing the joinings; for age does not tend to strengthen the feeble knees, and pipes are great sufferers from joint affections, no subject for wonder when one considers how often they are bent in surmounting roomattics. This caution becomes trebly necessary in dealing with the deciduous modern pipe. Modern builders think it sufficient to secure the top of each section alone, and leave the suspended lower end resting lightly on its supporting crest, ready to shift at a touch and yawn placidly in its attempter's face; the wall-fastenings also nowadays are insecurely embedded, and the pipe metal itself is of an inferior quality; lastly, worst crime of all, of late years the meagre pipes are often fixed directly against the wall and the "free-back prerogative" enjoyed by all the brotherhood for unnumbered ages, from the original member who performed before Moses to the great Peter Piper of Pickling fame himself, has been condemned. For all these reasons it is not possible for the climber to use mediaeval methods on the Victorian pipe, to "set his foot to the wall and his hand to the pipe and so throng up." He must proceed more scientifically, swarming with hand and knee directly up the pipe and reaching for the comparative security of the next wall-fastening for hand-hold from the relative insecurity of foot-hold on the one below: all strain upon the lower portion of each section must be as much as possible avoided, the climber first approximating his feet as near as possible to his hand-hold and then rapidly elongating himself until he attain the next collar, the ideal aimed at being the undulating motion of a caterpillar in a hurry*. Never more than one, at the most, should be on the sheer pipe together; for as Tacitus noticed with singular acumen: "Ruere ille non potest, ut hic non eodem motu labefactus concidat." For additional security, a rope should be employed which can be threaded backwards and forwards through each successive collar fastening, the lower end being secured or held below. To avoid the risk of the unroped gymnastics at each joint, some prefer to wear two lines, and thread them alternately, thus securing the protection of the one during the manipulation of the other. Others again employ a contrivance attached to the waist resembling a large pair of pincers, with which the metal can be gripped at need and the necessary rests secured for exhausted muscles.

---

* "Come per sostentar solaio o tetto / per mensola talvolta una figura / si vede giunger le ginocchia al peto." *Purg.* x.

This is called a 'hooker' and enjoys considerable popularity among pipe-cleaners*. There are few Circular pipes, be they free or close-backed, which cannot safely be negotiated with the aid of these safe-guards, but even these are of little avail in simplifying the Square pipe, as odious a subject as the clean-cut rock right-angle to its essayers. Mr Bernard Shaw condemns it in a classic passage:

> "Down *that* water-pipe! Stop! wait! I can't, I daren't! Climbing down the pipe means doing something." †

For the square pipe is always set close against its wall, and although the broad collars, usually roughened with the monogram of the brazen builder, give something of a hold, yet at the joints it is invariably rotten and its flat sides allow no insertion of finger, hooker or rope. Latin experts may have known of some pleasanter square variety, now extinct; it is difficult otherwise to appreciate Horace's criticism of one who

"aedificat, mutat quadrata rotundis."‡

Unfortunately in the modern form most commonly to be found in the Stone-building formation it adds materially to the other difficulties. It is unjustifiable as a rule to attempt it, except in those rare and pleasant cases where the shamefaced

---

* First mentioned in the works of Gildas Sapiens (6th cent.), chap. xix.: "The hooked instruments of their enemies (the Romans) were not idle on the wall."

† Arms and the Man I

‡ *Ep.* I. 100.

builder has concealed it in a chimney or funnel, when it proves a valuable assistance to a 'back-up' scramble and helps to lessen the large army of pipe-stoppers to whom this form of pipe is continually bringing the humiliation of being forced

> "To only eye their pipe
> And then to pipe their eye."

HOOD

If the water pipe follows the principles of the gully, the gut- GUTTERS ter is in all things to be treated like the ice-cornice which it so closely resembles. There are occasions when a fragile hand-hold can be obtained on an ice-fringe or a delicate traverse be made along the upper curve of an unnegotiable ice-slope, just as an old-fashioned wood or lead gutter can sometimes be trusted for a 'pull up' or a roof drain afford a risky passage, with sufficient aid from body-friction on the tiles*. But as a rule the law of the cornice should be the law of the gutter: "avoid when you can, and when you can't, break it down." If objections are made quote the law of parallels and demand precedents for prosecution of Alpine cornice-breakers. If this is insufficient, refer the homicidal gutter-supporters to that unanswerable indictment *"The Fallen Gutter-Percher, Bootless Musings o'er a Lost Sole."*

---

* Possibly Joab may claim to be the inventor of this method: "Tell my lord the king that I have fought, / And scaled, where the royal palace is, / The conduit heads." PEILE, *David and Bathsabe* I. 2.

TOWN
HOUSES The pipe and gutter take an additional and fictitious value from the fact that they are the only principles possessed and aired by the schismatic town builders, breakers of every law of Nature and the Tudors. Conceive for a moment the feelings of the enthusiast, as he ponders on those ranks on ranks of unrelenting cemented mansions, those vast wildernesses of brick and stone, utterly wasted for all useful purposes, unobserved of men and void even of form, save where some loose mortared Wall-flower may blush unseen, some dauntless Chimney-breast withstand the putty tyrants of Smithfields. We smile in derision when we read that the first law of the ancient state of San Marino forbids the citizens to climb the national walls. But which of our public buildings is open for the practice of man's competing hand or foot? Are not the laudable attempts of the from-time-to-time-inspired to scale their dwellings by the exterior balconies, the only royal route left to crowded cockneys, invariably frustrated by the police? What depths of suspicion do not attach to even an occasional recourse to a lamp post! It is illogical to complain of urban degradation when the only method of elevation is eliminated, and unlicensed builders are permitted to recline their tottering contracts one upon another in an infinite progression of inebriate dependence. Let us but have the courage of our convictions, we who profess consolation in wooden walls: let us enforce and extend our neglected building laws, follow Tacitus in his touching appeal for "aedificia non communione parietum

sed propriis quaeque muris,"* and compel every house to sit with its proper allowance of outside walls, pipes and cosy corners under its own roof-tree! Little need to marvel at the discontent of the "Knee-plus-knulltra" brotherhood, depicted in "*Saxifrage or Stonybroke* by *Housebreaker* [a Protest against a Growth in Jerry building]," when even the boldest, who worship wall-climbing "down to the ground," shrink frankly from the subterranean terrors of the urban area, and the most constant of mountain-resorters confess their timidity on the sides or summits of sun-scraping edifices:

> "Whose roofs too hot would prove for them all fire
> And walls too high for their unused pace"!
>
> CAMPION

In short though this region presents plenty of cause for rhetorical cussing, it affords very little material for practical discussing, and as a preferable course to accepting the linguistic Chiltern Hundreds, we will abandon the town building with the "Curse of Crum'le," and dismiss the town builder with the words of the sympathetic Isaiah, "Woe unto them that join house to house, till there be no place!"

The pipe and gutter lead naturally to the roof, of which the THE ROOF tile and the slate are the principal components and alone deserve special attention; for the flat leads with their "huge crag-platforms, smooth as burnished brass," so common in

---

* A. 15. 43

the great monasteries of the east, Patmos or Athos or the Meteora, may be neglected as too monotonous even for an unteachered school-treat.

TILES   The tile has it own artistic value:

> "Tiles and tile roofs have a curious way of tumbling to pieces in an irregular and eye-pleasing manner. The roof-tree bends its boughs a little under the weight, but yet preserves a sharpness at each end ... shattered here, cracked there, the tiles have an aspect of irregular existence,"
>
> JEFFERIES, *Open Air*

but this very irregularity and sharpness give it a greater value; for the tile is a very snow-clad ice-slope of delight*, rough to the hand and firm to the tread and granting at almost any angle to the india-rubber sole, unaided by the hand, a Grip unrivalled by Barnaby Rudge's. Sir Henry Wotton wished even to increase the angle for purposes of practice, and recommends "a graceful pendence of sloapeness," because "those climbs that have the lying of much snow (tile) ought to provide more inclining Pentinces."† The tile may crack occasionally beneath a heavy slipper but the injury is purely local and does not necessarily induce the human slipper's downfall: Antony in a

---

* Dante makes use of the same technical phraseology: "As snow that lies / Amid the living rafters." *Purg.* XXX

† *Elements of Architecture*

gable-glissade rather relished "per tegulas demitti"* It is not easy to discover what caused St Francis of Assisi's peculiar objection to tiles, and his conservative affection for wattle and mud, unless it were the recollection of some painful backsliding of this nature: "he went up," we read, "on to the roof of the house and bade the brethren go up also, and did begin to throw down to the ground the tiles wherewith the house was roofed" (Chap. viii.). The remonstrances, however, of the soldiers† of Assisi prevented, we are glad to learn, the entire destruction of their climb. The summit of a tiled gable is usually formed by a row of half drain-pipes, and where the angle is too steep to allow free running the so-called 'flat-foot' method, a sideways hand over hand walk, with the feet following each other flat upon the tiles, makes rapid progress possible. This is unsafe however, if the summit tiles, as frequently happens, are loose. In this case it is better to bestride the gable and walk with the hands along the ridge while the feet assist on either side. An ungraceful proceeding, true, and one which was not cordially practised by the great Victor Hugo: "Faire ces enjambées! cela ressemble à marcher sur l'arête d'un toit"; but it found enthusiastic supporters among the Romans:

---

* *Phil.* 2. A tile is sometimes intentionally removed to leave a foot or hand hold, and the practice is defended speciously as "step-cutting": "They undid a tile or two... / And up to the hall roof he stegth." *Seven Wise Masters* (14th cent.)

† Soldiers have always been conspicuous roofians on tiles: "Heus, quid agis tu, inquam, in tegulis, / Miles gloriosus?" PLAUTUS

> "Stalls, bulks, windows
> Are smothered up; leads filled and *ridges horsed.*"
> *Coriolanus II**

SLATES

All the snow is off when we come to the slates and this gilt-less gingerbread crackles and slimes beneath our feet, the very semblance of fragile and slippery ice. The dangers from this involuntary step-kicking do not however necessarily end, as in the case of the tile[†], with the injured bodily and mental feelings of the followers. Too often the verdict "it is a little rift within the roof" must be changed for "he broke an hole on heigh upon the gable," and veritable Agags may earn the title of stump socialists by unwittingly breaking the ice between two different strata of society[‡]. Here also, as on the tiles, the ridge or corona will be found the safest route, more especially as the angle of inclination upon slates passes earlier than on tiles into that of disinclination. The summit of the dormer window is an excellent 'take off,' from which the ridge may be reached with a rush, and the battlements are a great security in case of failure. We cannot do better than quote a few general hints on tectine principles from the antique but admirable work by Wallter Tiler on "Roofianism":

---

* The red-tiled roofs of many Hungarian and German towns yield noble scrambling: Martin Luther found their fascinations irresistible: "If there were as many devils in Worms, *as there are tiles on the roofs,* I would still go there."

† See first note, p. 24

‡ Note that the Latins called a "slater" *scandularius*

"Loke ye in gable empryse that ye sette ye stout rogue sans friends endlong on ye gablins, and let ye neist in Roguery overgo him overthwarts and stande upon his heid, and mo if needs most up-bounding till ye crowne be wonne; yet let not ye heighman grip hit rudely lest hit break and he that snatcheth atte ye crowne be locky if he have lefte an half. As ye Original Membere Chaucer sayeth:

> 'When they were alle on an hepe,
> Tho behind gonne uplepe,
> And clamben up on others faste,
> And up the nose on hyen cast,
> And trodden faste on others hedes
> And *stampe*,'

In sich wise sall ye lowest lichtly clomb, and ilke ye neist, and so on till ye foule chain be unbond and ye whilome bounderes be loose as afore*. If freindes polls be lacking an ashen pole y-clept an 'helping-stock' is stark enow. Ye poet Herbert telleth of certaine Philospheres who 'climbed with their staffs to heaven,' in good sooth a course extraordinaire and on preisent monteins and breeks unseemlike, yet mout it be they fonde them

'A newe unpossible cloude Kuckooburg,'

and doubtless they clomben up on ye lost matere y-clept 'Philosopher's Stone,' the which might wel surmount the Onseen, since in our yes hit surpasseth al belief! Likewise if on ye

---

* Gascoigne practised the same good method: "And make my backe a ladder for their feet, / To clyme the throne, wheron myself should sitte." *Steele Glas*

gablin ye wily chimney stack erect itself athwarts and yield ne ledge to feetes ne holde to hande, encompasse hit with rope, swingeing a stone at ye cordes ende, and so wriggle ronde. Unbounden climbe ye not, ne climb not alone; ye good fellowe Ecclesiast truly admonisheth 'two are bettere than one, for, fall they, one uplifteth his fellow anoon, yet woe to him that falleth alone for he nath ne fellowe him holpen*.' Hark ye too! If so be ye be assailed by hobgobblins and blue-deevils that dwell in ye house toppes, ne vaileth aught to Shoe hem off ne Hurl hem from you, then summon to aid ye Sherry-Cobbler or ye gentil Djin-Sling, ye veritable Spirits of ye Summit: this is my rede."

EXEGESIS With these few practical hints from an accomplished Roofian, whose usefulness will be found not to be confined alone to slaters and tilers, conclude the brief remarks on material and method. Brief, because he who has the true soul will soon obtain information from experience, and the true soul none can impart. The change of centuries has brought no cessation in the perennial pestering as to the nature of this climbing infatuation. The unenlightened still press with old-time pertinacity for a logical exposition of the instinct which induces rational beings to spread themselves over knobby countries or polish uncomfortable walls; mountaineers have long abandoned the attempt to answer, and wallers may imitate their

---

* *Eccles.* IV. 9

compassionate shrug. What philosophic system could congeal into frigid words the harmonious exaltation which drew the immortal Mr and Mrs Discobolus to "climb to the top of their Wall" and deliver thence that outburst of rapturous lyrical confession:

> "But now we believe it is better far
> To remain for ever just where we are!
> Far away from hurry and strife
> Here we will pass the rest of life
> Ding a dong, ding dong, ding!
> We want no knives, nor forks, nor chairs.
> No tables, nor carpets, nor household cares;
> From worry of life we've fled,
> O. W. X. Y. Z.,
> There is no more trouble ahead –
> Sorrow or any such thing
> For Mr and Mrs Discobolus!"
>
> LEAR, *Nonsense Verses*

For the benefit of the prosaic and yet unsatisfied research-student one superficial attraction is perhaps explicable, though its causal influence is psychologically questionable. The believers, whose "forms do pass on windows, and on roofs of marble palaces," are placed by the very practice of their art in contact with innumerable classes, granted even the communion of the immortals. Picture the clamorous delight of that 'obscure old bird' of a climber, on the occasion whose recollection drew from the indignant Shakespeare the suggestive lines:

PHILOSOPHY OF THE ART

"The night has been unruly, where we lay
Our chimneys were blown down, and, as they say,
Lamentings heard in the air, strange screams of death,
And prophesying with accents terrible
Of dire combustion; the obscure bird
Clamoured the live-long night!"

Macbeth

What is it to him that he has only saved his bacon with considerable injury, if his art has granted him to hear "dire combustion prophesied" of him by the "terrible accents" of an aroused Shakespeare!* Did not Chaucer suffer from a similar disturbance, and treat it with sympathetic forbearance?

"...They sat among,
Upon my chamber-roof without,
Upon the tyles, all about
And songen..."

Book of the Duchess

Roof-climbing leads the faithful one through the midst of great cities, of them but yet above them, ever observant from his lofty standpoint of his proper study Man, meeting with many and hearing possibly something new from most, preserving however like

"The feckless hairy oubit,

---

* Shakespeare apparently suffered on more than one occasion from this same enthusiast: "No jutty, frieze, / Buttress, or coign of vantage, but this 'bird' / Hath made his pendent bed."

His soul above the warkes o' creeping things."

KINGSLEY

No petty class distinction affects him. With unshaken calm he lingers alike above the heads of aristocrat and pauper. The only true socialist of his age, he views with impartial affection the prince's proscenium or the peasant's porch, the metal meeting house or the ruined monastery, pining with equal fervour to

"Tread Pride's golden palaces,
Or Penury's roofless hut and squalid cell."

CHATTERTON

and

"Drop from the charcoal-burner's hut
Or climb from the hemp-dresser's low shed."

By the Fireside

The necessary variety of "the personal adjustment to these heights" is a liberal education in itself, and there is additional charm in the very contrast of roof with roof and one householders temper with his neighbour's. The most peripatetic of modern Philosophers of the Porch expounds lucidly:

"The very difference piques!
Shows that e'en better than this best will be
This passing entertainment on a hut,
Whose bare walls take your fancy, since one stage more
And you arrive at the palace."

Sludge

With this one suggestive sop of pity for the non-climber, the

> "luckless turtle, fated
> Never to reach the summit of his shell!"
>
> *Persian Proverb*

the roof climber resigns himself to being relegated to the inexplicable. Nor does his philosophy fail him at the sound of the frequent invidious comparisons, drawn by the envious between mountain and wall. The Hill half-brothers shake too bombastic a finger of scorn to need the countercheck of a controversial fist:

MOUNTAIN
VERSUS WALL

> "(M.) What are those?
> Mere withered Wall-flowers, wavering overhead!
> They seem an elfish group with thin, bleached hair.
> That lean out of their topmost fortress! (R.) Look
> And listen, Mountain men, to what we say —"

namely that an all sufficient answer is rendered by the silent spread of the propaganda itself, effectively retorting upon the detractor,

> "Nunc cerne jugum discentia saxa,
> Intrantesque domos, jussumque recedere montem."
>
> STATIUS V. 58

Whatever the attraction of gorgeous colouring for the child, the appreciation of beauty of line is a later and more cultured taste. Many, who have returned year after year, babbling of green fields and blue mountains and bubbling over 'icy spires,' brown chalets and pink 'ambassadors from earth to heaven' find later a pleasing and unexpected stimulant to wearied eye and jaded hand in the soft grey outlines and clean-cut edges of our native architecture. Even old age, with its debarring of all more formidable ascents, wears a less hostile aspect in the company of such domestic consolations, and though it may be granted to few to have, with the indefatigable Alaric, "climbed his rock and scaled his town": —

> "Per tot montes urbesque cucurri,
> Fregi Alpes."
>
> CLAUDIAN V. 30

Or to be able to boast of the double and coincidental fulfilment:

> "I climbed the Roof at break of day,
> Sun-smitten Alps before me lay."
>
> *Dream of Fair Women*

Far less to share with the Pilgrim that first view of the Delectable Mountains from such an admirable standpoint:

> "When the morning was up they had him to the top of the house, and bid him look south: so he did and behold he saw at a great distance a most pleasant mountainous country."
>
> *Pilgrim's Progress*

Yet the gloomy rocks of our own dark gorges are vested with a twofold fascination for the well-balanced enthusiast, who loves to trace in their shadowy masses,

"The fretted pinnacle, the aisle, the nave.
All there, all scooped by Darkness from her cave."

Childe Harold

Or fancies he could discover

"Even in the crags at random flung.
That o'er the brawling torrent hung,
A bannered castle keep and tower
Return the lurid gleam.
With battled walls and buttress vast
And airy flanking towers that cast
Their shadow on the stream."

SCOTT, *Bridal of Triermain*

THE FUTURE   Of the developments of the future, who may speak? Perhaps even the Fraternity would hesitate to prophesy. Yet one word of anonymous forewarning may not be superfluous. Let the presently past contractor of today look well to the qualities of his work, and be it for each future ancestor to mark him with eagle eye and test him with sturdy foot. For if the signs of our times are more trustworthy than their structures, an era is again impending when the Roof and the Wall shall be put to their proper purpose, when, as of old:

"Videres *referta teda et laborantia*, ac ne eum quidem vacantem locum qui non nisi *suspensum et instabile vestigium* caperet."

PLINY THE YOUNGER, *Panegyric*

Then shall it be again but the daily routine that

"All are abroad to gaze,
Thick calf, fat foot, slim knee.
Mounted on Roof and Chimney"

Rejected Addresses

and the revolution of the cycles shall recall to us once more
that aspiring but vertiginous age, when

"All the city Walls were thronged on high.
And *myriads* to each giddy Turret clung!"

Revolt of Islam

SONG OF THE BROTHERHOOD

Sing we, brothers, in resonant chorus.
Paeans of praise to the ultimate goal.
Rolling its composite mountains before us,
Guide to the hand, yet support to the sole!
Heart-discloser! Brain-shelter of proof!
Brothers, hail to the region of Roof!

Wake, oh wake from Olympian portals
Echoes of joy for the fettered length,
Winning Prometheus-like for mortals
Roads to bliss in its iron strength!
Generous friendship's grandest type!
Chant we, brothers, the praise of the Pipe!

Last let our farewell unison render
Honours of song to the infinite Heart,
Which in its single, yet manifold splendour
Weldeth the myriad veins of our Art.
Thunder, Voice of our Climbing All,
Hail, all hail, to the world of the Wall!

BIBLIOGRAPHICAL

ROOF-TREE OF KNOWLEDGE

1. A volume of verse narrative, "*The Unpyed Piper's Pique and Gutter-Pipa Passes*"

2. "*Is Chimney-climbing sootable for Women?*" Published in connection with "*Cook's Tours on the Kitchen Range.*"

3. "*Cat-a-Walls, the Potentialities of 'Μή ού' in a Classic Construction*"

4. "*Investigation of the Pet-Alls of Wall-flowers and Verge-near Creepers.*"

5. Dormer's Classic Work on "*Attic Leanings and their Climbattic Causes*"

6. „AufRuf zum Teilnehmen" neue 'Ausgabe

7. "*Vane In-Spiration*" an old Murality Play, with its original Roof-Caste.

8. "*Feets on the Flats*" consisting of thirteen tall storeys.

9. "*For our Free-Dome*" against Fixed Spikes and Tied Houses, by a Lost Leader.

10. "*Railings without Tears*" First Steps for Children [with a key for parents, "*Sewing the Tares*"].

11. "*Know-ledge is better than Reach-is*" by the Last Man.

12. "*Sursum Corda! Our Bounden Duty*" a plea for the Rope.

13. "*Eaves-dropping*" by the Man in the Street.

APPENDIX A.

INTERIOR CLIMBING

> "A long table and a square table, or seats about the wall,
> *seem* things of form but *are* things of substance."
>
> BACON

Room-antic literature is too vast and its problems too varied for a complete summary, but a few practical suggestions may be found useful for rainy days, or for those whom circumstances or the builder have deprived of suitable exterior roofs and walls.

Every room offers its variety of problems greater or less in proportion to its furniture.

The Doorway. — This is invaluable for 'chimney' practice. It is the formation, according to Marvell,

> "Where larger-sized men may stoop
> To enter at the narrow loop.
> As practising in doors so straight"

— for the mountain gully. It admits of many variations of the 'back and knee' method in accordance with its width. The 'over door-ledge' makes a good 'finger traverse.' Ascents are frequently possible up panelled doors themselves by the bevelled edges or hinges. The poet Crabbe recommends these as an indispensable preparation for "Copper-horse" (see note p. 94) or Wall ascents. He relates how he "tried forty-nine doors,"

> "Before he mounted on the Brazen Horse,
> And o'er the Walls pursued his airy course."
>
> *The Happy Days*

The key is sometimes of use for a foothold; if that mysterious 'Lady Winde' of the familiar Nursery Rhyme, who

> "Went round about the house to find
> A chink to put her foot in;
> She tried the keyhole in the door,
> She tried the crevice in the floor.
> And drove the chimney soot in,"

had thought of putting the key *in*, she would not have been driven to such extremes as the fireplace for practice*.

The Window. — The ordinary narrow sill is a good balance traverse. Wide windows with deep embrasures afford excellent practice in the laborious 'foot and stretched arm' ascents. The shutter shares the merits of the door.

The Chair. — If solid possesses two uses; either, from the seat, clamber round the back, without touching the floor, or, a balance test, walk up the rungs of the back without the hands.

The Table. — Sitting on the edge, lower carefully with the

---

* Of a more expert lady, *Jesse Bourn*, Crabbe records how "He saw her *bending from the door.*"

hands, and pass under without floor-contact, ascending the other side of the leg*. The authenticated 'chimney climb' of a cake-seeking mouse, 'back and toe' between the double legs of a small tea-table, requires a special adaptation of the furniture for human beings.

The Sofa. — Set a few inches from the wall and balance-shuffle along the back. With increasing skill the distance from the wall can be diminished.

The Mantelpiece claims *Alice*[†] as one of its most enthusiastic exploiters, and Robert Burns fled on to it in moments of inspiration[‡]. The ready surmounting is unrivalled training for many kinds of rock-work. In climbing in large parties care must be taken to avoid the danger to those following of dislodging the ornament scree. Between the chimney breast and the return wall often lurks an attractive surprise camino.

Circuit traverses of most rooms can be contrived by adjustment of the furniture. The book-case and the door handle are important factors. That eminent Prime Minister, Cardinal Dubois, gained an undeserved reputation for insanity, equal to that bestowed by the Press on the early Alpine climbers, by being on several occasions discovered "making the circuit

---

* Chaucer however condemns this feat as ungraceful: "There saw I Coll Tragetour / Upon a table of sicamour / Play an uncouth thing to tell."

† Apparently she used to lead off from the grate: a loose foothold of hers *In Wonderland* brought Bill's chimney-climbing to a disastrous termination.

‡ See *Lines composed over the Chimneypiece.* His alternative refuge was a marble sideboard.

of his drawing-room on the furniture without touching the floor."

The Stair-case. – Most stair-cases are bordered by a wall or possess one free side. Ascend hanging by the hands alone from the edge of the tread, outside the baluster.

The Baluster. – With the back against the wall and the feet against the rail, a diagonal 'chimney' ascent is feasible. The landings are often a problem.

Good arm-exercise can be obtained by lying face down upon the rail and pulling up with the arms. More difficult is the accomplishment of the feat face upwards.

The Passages. – According to their breadth and the consistency of their walls offer many perpendicular 'back and toe' couloirs or longitudinal 'crab' traverses. They are often combined with corner and door ascents. A difficult fancy problem is for two climbers, back to back, to walk up the opposing walls. Spectators are warned against the danger of a lateral divergence of the thrust.

The Kitchen Pump. – An excellent and varied problem. Anatole France, we learn, "stimulated by the life of St Simeon Stylites, spent several hours a day climbing upon it." The tap and handle leakages afford good practice in waterfall scrambling and wet holds.

Where the natural configuration is faulty, artificial features can often be introduced at small expense.

For a free wall, a convenient contrivance requiring small

space is the Gabro-Wandboard; a sequence of stout planks some eight inches wide, fixed flat against the wall parallel to one another and two inches apart. Finger and toe climbs on the best Lake-school model, 'hands following,' 'hands together,' and 'hands alone,' can be multiplied to taste.

The small Jacobean oak panelling was this contrivance in its earliest natural form. The large useless Georgian panel took its place when the original object was lost through disuse. It was doubtless on the former that Cardinal Mazarin and the Count de Grammont decided their famous match as to "who could rush highest up the wall of the Cardinal's room."

Another complication suitable for drawing-room use is supplied by the Dolomite-Kaminboard, removable at pleasure. A robust two-inch plank, with a surface breadth of two and a half feet, is fixed upright facing the wall at a distance dictated by the climber's dimensions. The base is fitted with iron pegs, corresponding to sockets in the floor ordinarily hidden by the carpet. The top is supported from the wall by detachable bars. A second, narrower free-board can protect the wall paper, if thought necessary. Both must be from time to time roughened with a coarse file, and rubber-soled shoes are imperative. There are at least nine different methods of negotiating such an assisted formation, from the 'face and heel' wriggle, with the breast against the board, to the 'walk,' 'forward' or 'sideways,' one foot against either board and the body, balancing free to the rock, in the centre. Rugosities can be added to the back for 'technical' practice in 'pitch' problems. It has been suggested that by the simple mechanism of a string and a basket of stones useful experience might be obtained in the natural phenomenon of the avalanche, with a minimum of damage.

APPENDIX B.

HAYSTACK CLIMBING

> "*Then* when the Stacks get on their winter hap
> And thack and rape secure the toilwon crap — !"
> BURNS

In summer the enthusiast can disport himself on his mountains, his summer-houses and his dry walls, but in winter it might often seem oppressive to be confined perpetually to the stuffiness of interior practice. Consequently Nature has supplied a summit of purely winter growth in the haystack. Many neglect it, for the ragged exterior is obviously discouraging, but where the agricultural knife has shaped hard green walls and compact corners is the climber's opportunity, and an arrangement securing the cutter's co-operation can be guided to produce a world's desire of precipitous right angles, overhanging edge-aretes and sheer face-traverses. The method of attack is to drive the closed fingers up to the knuckles between the hay-strata in a slightly downward direction with the thumb a short distance below to assist the grip; the feet, shod with straight and sharp toed boots are similarly inserted with considerable force. Towards the summit — and this adds to the peculiar difficulty of hay-climbing — the fibre becomes looser, and additional security is given by clenching the hand inside the rift. Still higher, it is often expedient to thrust in the arm as far as the elbow.

The corner 'chimney' climbs are undoubtedly the easiest variety, as, by kicking steps sufficiently distant one on either side of the perpendicular angle, the strain upon the hands can be temporarily relieved. But the forcible sideways kick necessitated by the position needs considerable practice, as it has a tendency to incline upwards, and consequently to slip out under pressure.

The sheer face climbs or traverses are more severe, in that the strain upon the hand-muscles is continuous, and that even here the steepness of the angle makes a hard straight kick with raised knee difficult. Stack-walls also have a tendency to overhang slightly with their loose upper strata, as the Prior of Benethly discovered too late*, and they might prove a puzzle even to that eminent exponent Charles Cotton. He notes an ascent where that

> "appears
> Which the resemblance of a Haycock wears
> ...this doth still increase
> In height and bulk by a continual Drop
> Which, upon each distilling from the top,
> And falling still exactly on the Crown,
> There break themselves."
>
> *Wonders of the Peake*

---

* Matthew of Paris. "The rick being loosely built suddenly tottered and fell upon him!" The rest of the party escaped.

He implies that the debris of the cynically termed 'dropping' of climbers continually descending upon their craniums has magnified the 'bulk and height' of the ascent in common report. Very favourable structural conditions are necessary for complete success on the 'ridge' climbs up the right-angled corner edges. For normal anatomies, neither Quilps nor freaks, sideways and inwards hard kicking with feet and hands cannot be continued with comfort to a great perpendicular height, and if a slip has not preceded, a traverse is frequently the apologetic escape.

The secret of success, revealed by experience, is the never attempting long steps and keeping the arms well extended with the nose in the hay. The beginner, with hands secured, is tempted to lift the foot too high, and then, straightening up, finds himself unable to release either grip and retain his balance. Hands and feet should only rise a few inches at a time, hands leading, and keep their relative distance.

The early months of winter are the true stack season, when the hay has had time to settle and before its density has become unpleasant. Later and earlier in the year a flat spike affixed to the boot and leather or horn-tipped gloves are a convenience to save much finger-tip tribulation.

The real fascination of the hay-stack lies in the unique nature of its material, which adds to the pleasure of an arduous rock struggle the satisfaction of making, as on ice, all the holds and steps required. But the pleasure is paid for in physical fatigue. No type of climbing, admittedly, can compare with it in this respect. Twenty minutes of its convulsive clinging will force a pained resignation to the laws of gravity from most hands, and it is no uncommon sight to see a climber in the very act of surmounting the last cock of victory passively drop off from pure muscular exhaustion. As our learned precursor Bretton *all but* comments:

> "Haystack climbers have sudden falls."
>
> *Crossing of Proverbs*

And it is softer to pile up the precautionary truss before than after.

APPENDIX C

TREE CLIMBING.

"Never rejoice in the downfall of anyone: unhappy is he
who mistakes the branch for the tree."

The Talmud

This is no place to discuss the probable origin of tree climbing and the rights or wrongs of the Darwinistic theorem. It
is sufficient for a practical note that the antiquity of the art
is assured on either hypothesis. The tree played no unimpor-
tant part in Eden, and the modern Bandar-log preserves for
us a faithful picture of the manners of our alternative past.
Before the struggle for existence between man and man made
the Wall a necessity as a less assailable abiding place, the tree
had been the natural home of refuge from the assault of wild
animals. Presumably the now meaningless lullaby:

"Hush a bye, Baby, on the tree top!
When the wind blows the baby shall rock," etc.,

dates from this epoch, and has shared the fate of most of
the old nursery rhymes in long outlasting its applicability.
Under the artificial conditions of cultured humanity and
gardens these truths have lost their popularity; "rarely,"

Dante laments, "into the branches of the trees doth human worth mount up" (*Purg.* VII.). Yet the arboreal instinct is only dormant under artificial conditions and waits but an opportunity to declare itself in every human body. Place such a one once more among natural surroundings, and, as is apparent from *Robinson Crusoe* and the *Swiss Family Robinson*, his first idea is to start forthwith tree-climbing and bough-building. Study human nature in its least artificial present-ment. Among the South Sea islanders, "Tootoo," we read, "had built himself a sort of aerial baby-house in the pic-turesque tuft of a tree adjoining Marnego's habitation. He used to spend hours there, rustling among the branches, and shouting with delight every time the strong gusts swayed the flexible column" (*Typee*). The islanders' methods in tackling such columns, it maybe noted, "throwing the arms about the trunk, and pressing the soles of the feet against the tree, with legs horizontal and back arched," are worthy of further study. But it is not necessary to rummage so far as Absalom or the Boscobel oak for proofs of the universality of the desire. To every natural child it is as a second nature, and the main end of his aspirations and the chief terror of the gov-erness is invariably centred in the garden trees. The custom-ary parental attempt to check this inclination is much to be deplored, for the loss of the early climbing training of foot and head under the protection of the child's proverbial luck in these Alpine "nursery gardens" can find no substitute in later, stiffer life, when the nerves have come to their own. Many early educational experts, George Colman among them, regarded the tree as the inevitable precursor of the mountain. "O Saint Iago! May the man that falters to risk his neck on a mountain for a friend break it while he's a boy climbing for eggs in an orchard."* Trees are admirably suitable for child-climbing. The arrangement and form of the boughs, either out of reach and so impossible or, if reachable, excellent for holding, renders the line between the easy and the difficult unusually broad; and the capability of the muscles for a particular effort is the only decision left to the instinctive judgment of the child. By the occurrence of a rotten branch the caution and eclecticism so necessary in after-climbing are practically inculcated, and the lower branches are considerately contrived to break the force of the moral. Not improbably its kindergarten character in some degree accounts for the neglect of this branch of climbing by elder members. Yet the suspicion is irrepressible that the publicity of the performance under the frank criticisms of the past-masters of the nursery, present always in idea if not in person, shares the responsibility. The best of mountaineers may feel doubt of appearing to entire advantage under the novel conditions of swinging in a high wind from the end of a sixty foot pole. The discomfort, a real one to the tyro, of looking into space with either eye on each side of the

---

* *Mountaineers* III. 4

sole support, seems to have discouraged many historic arbo-
reans from calling attention to their attempts, and where
discovered in downfall they seek to pass it off with transpar-
ent euphuisms. "Under the greenwood tree, who loves to lie
with me?" is a typical and ready adoption on Shakespeare's
part — when surprised in an involuntary recoil — of Virgil's
sublime excuse "Mollesque sub arbore somni non absunt";
William Barnes frankly admits this timidity, when he

> "For merry pranks did crawl
> About the trees or broken wall...
> 'You can't climb down, old boy':
> 'I can, I'll bet — Heigh Hoy!'
> And down he fell — *you need not tell* —
> When we were young together."

The strict enclosure of parks at the present time is doubtless an intensification of the same feeling, but for all the zeal
of the owners it is regrettable to think how many noble trees
thus preserved for private consumption must fall ere they
contribute anything to the general knowledge of the subject.
We can but urge them as a body to emerge from behind their
walls and from under their branches and give the world the
benefit of their trees and their experience, in imitation of the
modern minor bard, whose sentiments do him credit:

> "Oh to cling to the swing of the tip-top cone
> In the blow and the blast of the frenzied Fohn!"

It would be of considerable profit were some sylvan scholar, more versed in the lately revived science of Forestry, to undertake the research into the preferences of earlier experts: to explain why Moschus chose the delights "ὑπὸ Πλατάνῳ βαθυφύλλῳ" or Horace those "sub antiqua Ilice"; why Jonah preferred the Gourd-tree for residence, or Deborah the Palm; what the village blacksmith saw in the Chestnut or Georgiana up her Gum-tree. To our limited experience some of the choices are inexplicable. True that the Oak, especially the Spanish variety, is an excellent training ground of strong curved branches and easy gradients – St Vincent of Paul, we are told, used as a child to "climb secretly into its branches" – and that the Chestnut perhaps comes nearest to our arboreal ideal with its short interspaces, frequent bifurcations and admirable upturned knobs on the trunk-base; but the Palm would seem formidable without artificial aids. As R. L. Stevenson apparently found – "Wouldn't it be aggravating to die under a cocoanut tree because you hadn't the knack of climbing it?" he writes; again the Gum-tree should be glutinous, and the Plane shares most of the demerits of the Beech, whose bare glassy stretches, down-trending excrescences and agonisingly acute-angled forks would make it a worthy choice for the tree-rambler's Hades. "The best tree to climb" – according to that greatest of nursery experts, Bevis – "was a larch... for the branches, at regular intervals, had grown on purpose for climbing." Many heavy-weights may not share this preference. It is easier to join in the universal Oriental affection for the Cedar. Many a knotty point may be found on its rugged trunk, to be solved only by its own rugosities, and on the firm green plates at the extremities of its boughs, pliantly sliding him from depth to depth, the victorious cone-winner can enjoy the rare exhilaration of an arboreal glissade.

It is customary among experts to slight the low summits of the Orchard trees. How mistaken a view this may be is shown by the escape of the famous Duc de Sully, whose knowledge of tree-value, it may be remarked also, often saved the great Henry's army. At the battle of Ivry, in spite of his armour and his seven wounds, he made such excellent progress up the "basses branches d'un poirier," that his less skilled enemies abandoned the pursuit in despair. Children should be encouraged to practise on them. How we should welcome the sight of our kindergarten teachers, in place of inculcating manual dexterity by patting clay models, expertly heading their infants in a follow-my-leader across a hazel or cherry copse!

Our forefathers cherished the Yew, and with due precautions as to eyes and cranium against its jagged points, many safe if rough scrambles can be evolved on its low levels. The Sycamore and the "Ash and the bonny Ivy-tree," so pined for by the north-country enthusiast, appear to us somewhat common-place, and in the last the cobwebs and the deceitful frailty of the holds are a frequent drawback. Critics differ as to whether the Ivy or the deciduous Cypress is to be held responsible for the 'backsliding' of Sir Thomas Wyatt:

> "For hitherto though I have lost my time,
> Me list no longer rotten boughs to climb."

But all our sympathies are with Miss Jane Austen in her admiration for the Evergreen*. There are few more varied pleasures than to ramble on some wet off-day across the length of a venerable shrubbery, swinging from branch to branch, breaking a path through the odorous fragility of the Acacia, bracing the grip on the slippery greenness of the Laurel or hazarding a leap across the low Holly-scrub to the well-earned rest on the sweet and sticky Lime-stump, with all the while the knowledge that a near depth of brown leaf and mossy refuse will soften the consequences of failure.

Many districts are blessed with a superfluity of Firs and nothing else. There is good climbing on all the Conifers, if the adhesive nature of the holding be nullified by strong gloves. A pleasant variation on the somewhat too easy ascents is to proceed by the arms alone, the feet being employed only as an occasional rest. The small higher branches are apt often to be found uncomfortably contiguous for a head-passage, and for ourselves we prefer to see all Fir branches cut close within two inches of the trunk. This however is a question of individual aesthetic taste.

---

* Mansfield Park

In tropical tree-ranges the hanging lianas are a most welcome assistance over the first twenty feet, and their place in our own country is occasionally filled by the drooping lengths of the Clematis. The Weeping Willow is negotiated in the same manner and, if we are to follow Marvell, affords equally excellent practice for the arms*. There has always been a romance attached to ascents on this tree since the days when the Exiles used to keep their harps each on his own Weeping Willow-top and ascending there at eve harp in mournful unison. Since the boughs often overhang the water, the descent is free from jars.

The problem as to the justifiability of climbing-irons has long been exercising the members of the craft. Many unarmable Pine trunks or brittle-twigged Poplars are certainly unnegotiable save by their means and the general adoption of the crampon by continental climbers would seem to be a precedent. The crampon, however, has never met with favour in this country, and we have to fall back upon the almost universal wearing of spurs in the hunting-field as our unique authority for this type of artificial holding on. It must be left to the nice sense of those who have experience of them to decide whether their employment is not an unwarrantable increase in the accompanying risks.

Another moot point is the question of tree formation. The hacking of steps in rock has always been tabooed, but on the

---

* Or to suspend my sliding foot / On the Osier's undermined root / And in the branches tough to hang. *Appleton House*

other hand fabricated climbing-boards are generally encouraged. Under which head tree-shaping may be placed is still an open discussion. Without pronouncing definitely, it has always seemed to us that the ideal beauty is attained in an admixture of utility, and that a scientifically lopped trunk, its boughs pruned into gratifying irregularities, and with interesting 'pitches' of bare interspaces allowing the eye to catch a glimpse of the commonly hidden graces of the stem, has all the interior charms of a theoretic climbing-ground and all the outward superiority of the clipped over the unclipped poodle.